FULF✠LLED

Uncovering the Biblical Foundations of Catholicism

SONJA CORBITT

ASCENSION

West Chester, Pennsylvania

Nihil obstat: Rev. Stephen Gideon
            Censor deputatus

Imprimatur: + Most Reverend J. Mark Spalding
            Bishop of Nashville
            February 22, 2018

Ascension
Post Office Box 1990
West Chester, PA 19380
1-800-376-0520
ascensionpress.com

Cover image (based on *Baptism of Christ* by Juan Fernández de Navarrete) and tabernacle illustrations: Jason Bach

Design: Rosemary Strohm

Printed in the United States of America

ISBN 978-1-945179-28-0

To St. Joseph, ex voto, for Bob.

CONTENTS

Called into His Presence

Introduction

*J*n my travels and interactions, I often hear how confused and flustered many Catholics feel when confronted with sincere questions from Protestants or fallen-away Catholics who measure the Catholic Faith against the Bible. Understanding the Faith accurately and concisely, especially in light of Scripture, has usually required cobbling apologetics material from multiple sources and authors—an arduous, confusing, and time-consuming endeavor.

Because of this inherent difficulty, many Catholics feel unable to defend the Catholic Faith and its practices with the Bible, while non-Catholic Christians can seemingly pick apart Catholic teachings with ease using the same Bible. It seems like Catholics and non-Catholics are speaking two different languages within the same book. As a result, Catholics' faith-sharing goes unheard, and under such passionate dismissal, they feel defeated and even question the veracity of their own faith. Many fall away entirely.

This reality is as intolerable to me as a fresh burn, one that I will work until my last breath to help alleviate as a matter of sweet penance. I was a non-Catholic who once made it her mission to "pick off" Catholics from the Church, and I was very good at it.

I used the "Roman Road" like a rapier:

- "There is none righteous, no, not one" (Romans 3:10).

- "All have sinned and fall short of the glory of God" (Romans 3:23).

- "The wages of sin is death, but the free gift of God is eternal life in Christ Jesus our Lord" (Romans 6:23).

- "If you confess with your lips that Jesus is Lord and believe in your heart that God has raised him from the dead, you will be saved. For man believes with his heart and so is justified, and he confesses with his lips and so is saved" (Romans 10:9-10).

Did you see anything there about sacraments? It says *believe* and *confess,* and you will be saved. Confession to a priest? The Bible does not say that anywhere, and the Bible does not lie. Church attendance? Saints? Holy days of "obligation"? None of these are in the Bible either. You must accept Jesus and be saved; that is all. You just read it yourself. Have you been saved? Will you go to heaven when you die? "For God so loved the world that he gave his only Son, that whoever believes in him *should not perish* but have eternal life" (John 3:16, emphasis added). You must be saved or go to hell and perish. It is that simple ... or so I thought.

When my understanding of the Catholic Faith "clicked" (largely because of my understanding of the information I share in this book), I spent the long, dark hours of an entire night on my face before the Lord, sobbing at my zealous, self-righteous ignorance in leading people away from his Church—to the "valley of dry bones," where the living breath of the Holy Spirit in the sacraments does not blow (see Ezekiel 37).

Writing these words brings tears all over again. With my head, heart, and faith now fulfilled in the Church, I see with painful regularity how quickly God's people are "destroyed for lack of knowledge" (Hosea 4:6), even as they yearn to share the beautiful practices that animate their lives with those they know and love.

I know you long to be able to explain the glorious, ever-ancient, ever-new Catholic Faith in a way that will not only intrigue but also inspire others to investigate and embrace the Church more fully.

Since I was once an adversary of the Church, by God's gracious mercy I know how to answer this longing. I have begged God to give me back every Catholic I helped steal away from the Faith, number by number, and to make me an instrument in the Church for unity.

Fulfilled: Uncovering the Biblical Foundations of Catholicism is designed to equip you to share your faith concisely. You will discover the Old Testament Tabernacle as the perfectly packaged biblical model for conveniently understanding and explaining Catholic beliefs and practices, some of which baffle non-Catholics and Catholics alike.

The goal of *Fulfilled* is to help you acquire a thorough knowledge of the Tabernacle's design, facilities, and function as the blueprint for the fullness of faith we live in Christ and his Church. You will come to appreciate how the Catholic Liturgy is the fulfillment of the pattern followed in the Old Testament Tabernacle.

You will come to appreciate the Catholic Faith we profess and live as the fulfillment of the pattern followed in the Old Testament Tabernacle. There are special features at the end of each chapter to help you connect your faith and the practice of it with the Old and New Testaments. These include:

- A **Review:** Since "repetition is the mother of learning," we briefly revisit the main points of each chapter.

- An **Invitation,** which applies the Scripture passages and the themes presented in the chapter to your life. *Note: This book quotes from the Revised Standard Version – Catholic Edition (RSV–CE) of the Bible.*

- A **God Prompt – LOVE the Word**™ exercise that will help you practice getting in touch with God directly and personally.

The goal of this book is to arm you with a new apologetics resource and teach you how to answer false—or at least incomplete—interpretations of Scripture with the fullness of Catholic history and teaching. It is my hope that you will no longer be intimidated by a lack of information and will be equipped with a clear, convenient way to communicate the truths of the Faith in light of Scripture.

The Bible, the glorious book we share with non-Catholic Christians, contains the blueprint of our whole, living Faith. This Tabernacle faith-sharing model gives you a starting place in Scripture that will help you claim souls for God's Church. I have passionately sought this important moment with you, and many prayers have preceded you here. Let's get started!

A Home for God

Old Testament Tabernacle Worship:
Fulfilled in the Catholic Church

*W*hen I was a Protestant, worship in my church on Sunday looked like this: a welcome and announcements; an uplifting hymn sung by the entire congregation; a pastoral prayer; another congregational hymn; the offering; a song, hymn, or other piece of sacred music sung by the choir; a sermon; an "invitation" to live out what was preached; and a closing prayer of blessing.

Regardless of its style or content, the worship service always consisted of about fifteen minutes of singing and forty-five minutes of preaching. Every Protestant worship service I ever participated in followed this traditional format, even when "contemporary services" came on the scene.

Many Protestant churches added an earlier service to accommodate those who preferred a "contemporary" worship style. Sometimes these included drama, dance, painting, mime, bells, and other techniques to illustrate what was being preached that Sunday. (I once attended a service during which the pastor broke a huge mirror with a sledgehammer to emphasize a particular point of his preaching!) Contemporary Sunday services typically featured a praise band that performed modern worship songs from a stage equipped with concert lighting, a large projection screen for song lyrics, slide shows, and compelling videos. If you have never attended such a service, you may have seen something similar on TV. They are compelling and heart-soaring and can be furiously inspiring, emotional, and worshipful.

But this is no different than anything in a local arena. There is no "holy other" about it, no mystery, no silence, no stillness, no peace. Eventually, it felt vain to me. Worship in nearly all Protestant churches, then, is primarily centered on the Sunday service, with emphasis on praise and prayer. In the Old Testament, however, God prescribed worship as an entire communal way of life, centered around the Tabernacle where God's presence "lived." Tabernacle-centered worship occurred every day, as well as on seasonal and annual feasts.

As a non-Catholic, the more I learned about Tabernacle worship in the Old Testament, the more I wondered why God would specify such worship so carefully—and hold his people to following it so strictly over many generations—if New Testament worship was not supposed to resemble it in any way. And the heavenly worship described in Revelation looked *nothing* like the worship in my church. In fact, my worship service was missing almost all of the elements prescribed in the Bible—but it did sometimes resemble the time in the New Testament when St. Paul's preaching was so long-winded that Eutychus drifted to sleep after midnight and fell out a window (see Acts 20:9)!

God is not arbitrary; he does not change (see Malachi 3:6). If Old Testament worship was preparation for New Testament and heavenly worship, shouldn't there be some similarity between them?

Over time, I came to see that this similarity exists in the Catholic Church, in the Mass. In fact, it is only in the Catholic Faith that *all* the elements of biblical worship are fully—not just symbolically—maintained. This does not mean, of course, that the worship of non-Catholics is not pleasing to God; any worship is pleasing to him if it is sincere. But any worship less than what God prescribed for us lacks a great deal of what draws us most deeply into his presence.

The Old Testament shows us that God *loves* law and ritual! In fact, God was adamant about the Israelites maintaining strict obedience regarding worship, specifically so its fulfillment in the Church would be recognizable to us—and so that the eternal worship in heaven would be familiar to us as well.

Catholic rituals and practices can sometimes seem old fashioned, outdated, or even unbiblical at first glance. But the form of the

Catholic Liturgy has been prescribed by God himself, rooted in the Old Testament Tabernacle, modeled after the worship occurring eternally in heaven, and reflected in our souls.

We know what kind of worship pleases God and draws us fully into his presence because he told us what it should look like in the Old Testament Tabernacle and in prophecies of the new Temple. Because Old Testament worship was modeled after heavenly worship, we see that proper New Testament worship should also somehow follow the Tabernacle's structure and order—not as a dead skeleton, but as a living, breathing, fleshed-out practice that actually communicates the grace within it.

The first five books of the Bible, the Pentateuch or Torah, reveal God's desire and prescription for worship. Here, we can discern some wonderful things about how our unchangeable God interacts with his people, even today.

CALLED TO THE MOUNTAIN

In Exodus 3:18, God sends Moses to Pharaoh to request that Pharaoh grant the people a three-day "leave of absence" of sorts, so they could go into the desert and offer sacrifices to him. Exodus is very much the story of Moses' repeated confrontations with a stubborn Pharaoh. Ultimately, because he would not allow God's people to go and worship for a few days, God removed his people from Pharaoh's rule completely.

In Exodus 19:1-2, after the Israelites have gone out from Egypt, they make a "pit stop" on the way to the Promised Land at Sinai (also called Horeb), God's holy mountain—the very same mountain upon which Moses received God's command at the burning bush to lead his people out of Egypt (see Exodus 3:1–4:17).

The Exodus had "drawn" the Hebrews out of Egypt under the leadership of Moses, whose name means "to draw out." God then brings his people to himself at Sinai, and they become a nation with which he will make his covenant. If they obey him and keep the covenant, God promises to make them his special treasure (see Exodus 19:3-6). He promises to lavish special knowledge and attention on them and make them a kingdom of priests and a holy nation. His Chosen People will be in a unique relationship with him, different from every other nation because of their relationship with the living God. Every other nation will learn of God through them, and they will lead others to worship him—not just through Temple ceremonies but through an entire way of life.

The people readily agree and prepare to meet God at Sinai, where he will speak audibly to Moses so that the entire nation will know God is present. In anticipation of meeting God, they were required to make special preparations. And then ...

> On the morning of the third day there were thunders and lightnings, and a thick cloud upon the mountain, and a very loud trumpet blast, so that all the people who were in the camp trembled. Then Moses brought the people out of the camp to meet God; and they took their stand at the foot of the mountain. And Mount Sinai was wrapped in smoke, because the LORD descended upon it in fire; and the smoke of it went up like the smoke of a kiln, and the whole mountain quaked greatly. And as the sound of the trumpet grew louder and louder, Moses spoke, and God answered him in thunder. And the LORD came down upon Mount Sinai, to the top of the mountain; and the LORD called Moses to the top of the mountain, and Moses went up (Exodus 19:16-20).

Read this passage again, slowly. Imagine that you are one of the Israelites present at Sinai. I am not sure why this brings tears to my eyes, except that I want to be there, keeping my eyes tightly shut the whole time, praying not to be annihilated by the glorious tornado of unbearable, thundering holiness whirling around that mountain. Alleluia! We can understand the terror the people of Israel must have felt; they knew from the patriarchs that no one could look upon God's face and live. But surely, we must not say we share their ultimate desire, as they refused to come near God again for fear (see Exodus 20:18-21).

Yet here was the Almighty, the King of the Ages, the Lord of Hosts coming to commune with them. They trembled in one accord, saying, "Let me not hear again the voice of the LORD my God, or see this great fire any more, lest I die" (Deuteronomy 18:16).

Never were the people so unified in their desire, and never was a nation so fearful. The fear of God abounded in the heart of everyone present. Each was made to know that he or she was unclean before God, so they spoke as one, asking that Moses be their mediator. God's Word would be given to them through Moses, as he had done before in the Exodus events. Imagine if they had said, "I don't need Moses! God is my only mediator!" and begun the hike up the mountain into the flaming, thundering, quaking cloud.

CALLED FOR RELATIONSHIP

On the top of Mount Sinai, with the people awaiting his return at its base, Moses received the formal covenant from God. The next twelve chapters of Exodus include the Ten Commandments and the instructions for constructing the Tabernacle, followed by the ceremonial law—"worship manual," if you will—in Leviticus.

In striking contrast to the ten plagues, we are told in Exodus 31:18 that God gave Moses the gift of the Ten Commandments. On stone tablets, written by the "finger of God," he made a "keepsake" for the people. I find that to be a very tender thought. We also find this type of intimate terminology for the written Word of God in the New

Testament. In 2 Timothy 3:16, we read that "all scripture is *inspired by God*" (emphasis added). "Inspired" here literally means "God-breathed."

With his "breath and finger," God wrote us a love letter of sorts, an invitation to risk everything with him. The Bible is the epic story of how determined God is to draw us to himself and give himself to us as fully as we will allow. By reading the Bible, we can know when we are worshiping in a manner that allows for a complete self-donation. As St. Paul says in his second letter to Timothy, "All scripture is inspired by God and profitable for teaching, for reproof, for correction, and for training in *righteousness*" (2 Timothy 3:16; emphasis added). Simply put, "righteousness" means "what is right."

At Sinai, Moses was called by God to lead the nation of Israel into "right worship." It was on this same mountain that Moses received the Ten Commandments and the whole Law (or Torah) through which he would instruct the people in proper worship through the Tabernacle that would be built at its base. As the *Catechism of the Catholic Church* (CCC) states:

> The gift of the Commandments is the gift of God himself and his holy will. In making his will known, God reveals himself to his people. The gift of the commandments and of the Law is part of the covenant God sealed with his own (CCC 2059–2016).

Moses placed himself at God's service—and he was faithful. He led the new nation of God to the mountain to which God had called them to begin to live together in relationship. The people of Israel would memorialize and remember this event forever.

A HOUSE MADE OF GIFTS

God led his people out of bondage to meet and worship him on Mount Sinai. It was a terrifying experience and one they never forgot as a people. The rest of the book of Exodus is the account of what occurred on Mount Sinai and the instructions Moses was given. The instructions include the laws and Ten Commandments, a liturgical worship schedule, worship procedures, and the elaborate, detailed instructions for the Tabernacle and its furnishings. Skilled workmen carried out the important task of building everything. The Tabernacle was the center of the communal life of God's people.

After leading his Old Testament people out of Egyptian slavery, God told them, through Moses, that he desired to live with them. Think about that for a moment. The same God who created photons, fingerprints, and moose, wants to live and remain close to you. The word "tabernacle" literally means "to dwell." The instructions God gave to Moses on Mount Sinai contained detailed plans for a physical worship structure that would be God's new "home" in the midst of his people:

> Speak to the people of Israel, that they take for me an offering; from every man whose heart makes him willing you shall receive the offering for me ... And let them make me a sanctuary, that I may dwell in their midst. According to all that I show you concerning the pattern of the tabernacle, and of all its furniture, so you shall make it (Exodus 25:2, 8-9).

Before they left Egypt, the people were given spoils—gold, silver, jewels, thread, and textiles—everything they would need to construct the Tabernacle God was planning. God wanted his new home to be made from offerings given to him by his people from those spoils. Consider that when harassed by thoughts that your life has been too sinful for God to ever be able to use.

Whatever gifts individuals might give for the purpose, God would show the nation exactly how to use them to make his new Tabernacle. As a Catholic, the term "tabernacle" probably makes you think of the place in your church that houses the ciborium containing the Blessed Sacrament. But I would like you to think of the Tabernacle in several other distinct ways.

The first is the Old Testament Tabernacle. Throughout history, the Tabernacle was the outward sign and reminder of God's desire to be surrounded by his people, to be present with and to live among them as the heartbeat of their existence.

It was a tent of sorts and the portable place of worship for the nomadic Israelites who lived directly outside its gates. Their campsites surrounded the Tabernacle by tribe on all sides in a picture of perfect design and order in what seemed like chaotic wandering in the wilderness. God placed each Israelite tribe in a specific position facing the Tabernacle (see Numbers 2). The camp was divided into four sets of three tribes at each compass point with one flag for each tribe.

Because a person's identity was derived from his or her tribe and position in relation to the Tabernacle, the tribal organization offered security to the Israelites in their relationship to the living God who dwelt there. Sometimes in Scripture, the term "tabernacle" indicates the whole Temple area. Other times it refers to the tent sanctuary itself. This was the layout of the sanctuary:

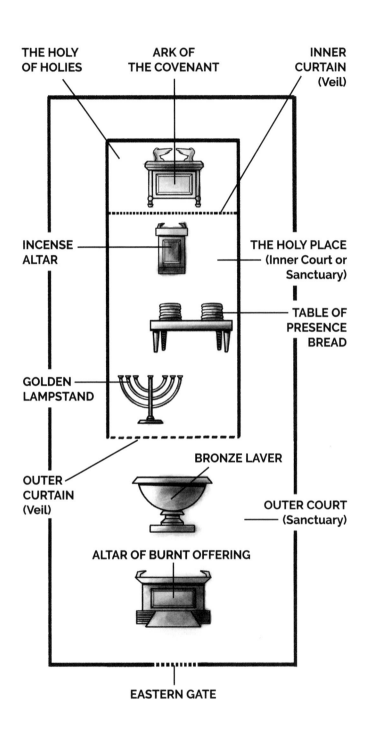

THE HOLY
OF HOLIES

ARK OF
THE COVENANT

INNER
CURTAIN
(Veil)

INCENSE
ALTAR

THE HOLY PLACE
(Inner Court or
Sanctuary)

TABLE OF
PRESENCE
BREAD

GOLDEN
LAMPSTAND

OUTER
CURTAIN
(Veil)

BRONZE LAVER

OUTER COURT
(Sanctuary)

ALTAR OF BURNT OFFERING

EASTERN GATE

Through the Tabernacle, God would teach a people accustomed to pagan Egyptian worship how to worship the One True God properly. They were not yet, nor for long afterward, capable of the concept of a God who "does not dwell in houses made with hands" (Acts 7:48), so a temple was given to them, but not fixed to one spot.

Instead, its removal from place to place in the nomadic life of the Israelites offered a persistent education leading away from the polytheism of their enslavement. The Tabernacle included some fascinating facilities. Let's get a general picture.

THE COURTYARD

Located in the outer courtyard, just inside the gate, was a grill-like structure for ritual burnt offerings. The daily animal sacrifices offered on the altar were a constant reminder that sin causes death, and that atonement is the first requirement for entering into the presence of God.

The next worship element was the bronze laver full of water, an oversized birdbath-shaped structure used for washing the blood and dirt off the priests' hands and feet before they entered the enclosed sanctuary for their ministry duties (see Exodus 30:18-20, 40:30-32). The constant washing taught the people that after atonement for sin, purity was necessary to draw near to God in the sanctuary.

THE SANCTUARY

Just inside the thick outer curtain protecting the sanctuary of the Tabernacle, it was cool and dim. Incense hung in the air as the priest went about his duties in the glow of the man-sized golden menorah to his immediate left.

The priest was responsible for keeping the seven oil lamps of the menorah full of oil and their wicks trimmed at all times. The gold Table of Presence Bread was located to the right, opposite the lampstand, while the incense altar stood straight ahead, in front of another thick, more richly embroidered curtain. The twelve loaves of Presence Bread, also called Bread of the Face (of God), represented the twelve tribes of Israel, and the priest kept the bread fresh and replenished on a weekly basis. The bread was called Presence Bread because it was placed in the presence of God, and God was present in it, in the Tabernacle.

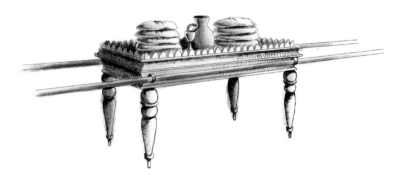

The incense altar was a smaller version of the outdoor sacrificial altar, and a special formula of incense burned perpetually. Altogether, these elements of sanctuary furniture communicated that light, sustenance, and prayer are found in the presence of God.

THE INNER SANCTUARY, THE HOLY OF HOLIES

Just inside the inner curtain separating the Holy Place from the Holy of Holies was the Ark, the most sacred of all the furniture in the Tabernacle, because it was here on which the presence of God rested in the pillar of fire and cloud. Inside the Ark, the Hebrews kept a copy of the Ten Commandments to summarize and symbolize the unsurpassed gift of the whole Law; a memorial pot of the daily manna from heaven to stress God's faithful daily provision; and Aaron's budded rod to remind them they lived under the protective authority of an institutional priesthood, all of it according to the explicit instruction and will of God.

Everything in the Tabernacle was specified by God himself to Moses, down to the last detail. The weight of all the gold used in the construction of the Tabernacle is thought to be about one ton! As mentioned, the gold and silver and brass, all the jewels and linens—everything needed to construct and decorate the Tabernacle and its furnishings according to God's instructions—was provided by God from their enemies and slave masters, the Egyptians.

> The people of Israel had also done as Moses told them, for they had asked of the Egyptians jewelry of silver and of gold, and clothing; and the LORD had given the people favor in the sight of the Egyptians, so that they let them have what they asked. Thus they despoiled the Egyptians (Exodus 12:35-36).

Whatever you have suffered can also be turned into the treasure that will furnish and decorate the sanctuary of your heart.

Although it was a tent and portable, the Old Testament Tabernacle was not a substitute dwelling, but a glorious shrine that symbolized the presence of God living in the midst of his people. The Tabernacle was the "how" of the Old Testament people, the locus of their communal life and worship. All the seasons and liturgical festivals of the year centered around it, especially the sacred family meal of Passover when the Passover lamb was offered on the altar of burnt offering every spring.

Perhaps most importantly, the Tabernacle was a copy of the sanctuary in heaven and the prototype of the Church to come: "They serve a copy and shadow of the heavenly sanctuary" (Hebrews 8:5). The reason God specified the Tabernacle, its liturgical worship, and its elements in such detail to Moses in the Law at Mount Sinai is because it was patterned after the one in heaven and would be the pattern, fulfilled, for New Testament worship.

WORSHIP IS NOT ABOUT ME

In Scripture, we see that God desires a particular kind of worship. That means that worship is not about me, what I like, or whether I am being entertained or satisfied by what is happening. I love how beautifully Robert Cardinal Sarah emphasizes this point:

> God, not man is at the center of Catholic liturgy. We come to worship him. The liturgy is not about you and I; it is not where we celebrate our own identity or achievements or exalt or promote our own culture and local religious customs. The liturgy is first and foremost about God and what he has done for us.[1]

C.S. Lewis clarifies that the Liturgy is the entry point to God's presence, "In commanding us to glorify him, God is inviting us to enjoy him."[2]

My friend Deacon Harold Burke-Sivers likes to say that if you are "not being fed" at Mass, it is because you prefer junk food, and you do not get junk food at Mass. Worship is about God, what he wants, what glorifies and reveals him most, and what draws us into the closest possible proximity to him in heaven. God knows exactly what leads us most deeply to intimacy with him. For these reasons, God also specified in great detail how the Tabernacle should be built, filled, and used. He strictly held their generations to its adherence for our benefit, so we could recognize and participate in it similarly.

Proper worship was meant to include liturgy, ritual, and ceremony. The Old Testament Tabernacle included a priesthood, an altar, an altar fire, a water basin, a light source, bread and wine, incense, a special curtain, a throne for God, a liturgy, and a liturgical schedule. Each of these things was required for proper worship, according to God and specified by him. In addition, each element was required to remain, perpetually, throughout the generations of his people (see Exodus 25–31); and they do remain with God's people—in, with, and through Christ.

THE DIFFERENCE BETWEEN "ABOLISHED" AND "FULFILLED"

In the Old Testament, this Tabernacle was the visible symbol and reality of God's presence with his people. In the book of Hebrews, we see the historical Jewish association of the Tabernacle with the cosmos, the holy and most holy divisions (sanctuary and Holy of Holies) representing the earthly and heavenly realms of Christ's activity. We will explore this idea more closely in the next chapter.

Scripture scholars have long debated why the book of Hebrews repeatedly refers to the Old Testament Tabernacle rather than the later, grander Temple of Solomon, which is said to symbolize the new creation. Perhaps, as many think, the Temple was already destroyed by the time the book of Hebrews was written, illustrating the book's purpose for encouraging the new Christians to cling to their better Tabernacle and High Priest in Christ.

In any case, beyond its literal application as the worship place of the nomadic Jewish people through the wilderness, strict Hebrew treatment of the Tabernacle focuses in metaphors for the cosmos in this way, or for the highest heaven beyond the cosmos, and ends there for lack of a Messiah. Because their Scripture—our Old Testament—makes this connection to the cosmos, it illustrates why the Old Testament Law and its Tabernacle can never be "abolished" until "heaven and earth pass away," as Jesus said in Matthew 5:18.

Christian denominationalists also illustrate the fulfilled-not-abolished principle without realizing it, in expending vast amounts of energy exploring the symbolism and imagery of the Tabernacle as the sacred spiritual "space" in which Jesus as the heavenly High Priest makes spiritual, eternal atonement for sin. But they necessarily stop all consideration with Jesus in heaven, declaring the Old Testament "obsolete" (Hebrews 8:13), abolished, in the same way Herod's temple was sacked and burned to the ground in AD 70 and never rebuilt. If Christ's sacrifice destroyed the earthly sacrificial system, then it is only logical that an earthly New Testament sanctuary is also unnecessary.

But if he *fulfilled* the earthly sacrificial system ... well, that is an entirely different idea altogether. Jesus himself, the fulfiller and fulfillment, is not obsolete in the way Herod's temple is extinct, likely never to be rebuilt. Rather, Jesus' body, as the true and eternal Temple, was bludgeoned, ripped open, pierced, and crucified but rose from the dead completely different and new and lives on through his people. Jesus lives on, the "system" lives on. Similar, but different. Not Jewish. And in a resurrected way that fully incorporates his "old," "obsolete" body, yet infuses and communicates life and grace.

My point is that the Old Testament worship system was not abolished as a mistake or failure any more than Jesus' earthly body was wiped out as a mistake or failure. Jesus' body was dead and resurrected. The Old Testament Law was dead and resurrected in him and with him as the glorious blueprint for fulfillment—for proper, later worship in Christ. Simply, the Tabernacle teaches us what true worship looks like, here and in heaven.

The Jews were not shown the plenitude of its eventual purpose as type and shadow at Sinai, so they received the Law as the gift of revelation from God that it was, embracing it with great joy and reverencing its splendor throughout their generations, even to this day. And if that Law "carved in letters on stone, came with such splendor that the Israelites could not look at Moses' face because of its brightness, fading as this was, will not the dispensation of the Spirit be attended with greater splendor?" (2 Corinthians 3:7-9).

The Old Testament Tabernacle and Law surrounding it did exactly what they were designed to do. Scripture teaches in divine pedagogy: that Old Testament Law—summarized in the Tabernacle—was the template and tutor for New Testament law and therefore necessary for establishing the foundation of the Church as it is supposed to function, according to the book of Hebrews. The Torah was not designed to communicate grace, only to tutor and prepare humanity to receive grace in some resurrected way.

Jesus brings a new law on a new mount, one that does not eliminate the old, but wraps it up in an embrace and *includes* it in its minutiae by diving beneath the surface of our outward behavior to the inward motivations beneath.

> Whoever then relaxes one of the least of these commandments and teaches men so, shall be called least in the kingdom of heaven; but he who does them and teaches them shall be called great in the kingdom of heaven (Matthew 5:19-20).

The sacrificial system is transformed in him, High Priest and Victim, and in us as his mystical body, who follows him in all things. Like him, we consecrate ourselves to God as living sacrifices through a prescribed worship system. This, and only this, is true "spiritual worship" (Romans 12:1).

Because it was a copy of the tabernacle that eternally exists in heaven, God was very specific about how everything should be made and situated:

> They serve a copy and shadow of the heavenly sanctuary; for when Moses was about to erect the tent, he was instructed by God, saying, "See that you make everything according to the pattern which was shown you on the mountain" (Hebrews 8:5).

Later, the more permanent temples of Solomon and Herod, for which the Tabernacle was the temporary prototype, retained all the attributes of the portable Temple of Exodus, but enjoyed more lavish decoration and the stability of stone construction. But it was not until "the days were completed" that we get an inkling of what God was ultimately up to, something unheard of and spectacularly new. In addition to the Old Testament worship structure, Mary is another way I would like you to think of the word "tabernacle."

THE FIRST HUMAN TABERNACLE

In Luke 1, we read the stunning news that a human being—Mary—will be a tabernacle for God:

> And the angel said to her, "Do not be afraid, Mary, for you have found favor with God. And behold, you will conceive in your womb and bear a son, and you shall call his name Jesus ... therefore the child to be born will be called holy, the Son of God" (Luke 1:30-31, 35).

I have always found this account fascinating, partly because God tells Mary how pleased he is with her, and I long to hear those words from him myself. I am also captivated by Mary's reaction: "And Mary said to the angel, 'How can this be, since I have no husband?'" (Luke 1:34). Has God ever revealed something to you that you could not comprehend in the moment?

At the Annunciation, the Virgin Mary is told that the power of the Holy Spirit will "come upon," or "overshadow," her (Luke 1:35). That almost makes me shiver. In the Septuagint, the Greek version of the Old Testament, the language is the same as that in Exodus 40:34-35:

> Then the cloud covered the tent of meeting, and the glory of the LORD filled the tabernacle. And Moses was not able to enter the tent of meeting, because the cloud *abode upon* it, and the glory of the LORD filled the tabernacle (emphasis added).

This most sacred moment in human history is the Incarnation, and it is why we bow deeply during the Mass at the words of the Nicene Creed, "By the Holy Spirit was incarnate of the Virgin Mary, and became man." It is the moment when Mary's Creator is conceived within her, the moment when the New Covenant takes flesh within Mary, who is called the "Ark of the New Covenant" by the Church Fathers. *Glorious. Marvelous. Miraculous.*

For this reason, Mary is also given the title *Theotokos* by the Church, meaning "Mother of God." And it is at this moment that Mary becomes the very first living tabernacle. She is the living temple in whom the Son of God, the Second Person of the Trinity, makes human nature the "house" in which he dwells. The tabernacle of his flesh is formed wholly from hers.

God was really present in the Old Testament Tabernacle, in the pillar of cloud and fire, leading his people. He was really present in Mary at the Incarnation. The first thing she and Joseph do with the new baby, as obedient Jewish parents, is to present Jesus in the Temple according to Jewish Law. There, they ascend the Temple stones in Jerusalem, summing up the Old Testament and ushering in something wonderfully new—something similar to the old but fresh, vibrant, and mercifully new.

JESUS, THE TRUE AND FINAL TABERNACLE

Thousands of years after the original Old Testament occupation of the cloud and fire in the Tabernacle, the Gospel of John applies a particularly special designation to the new way God is present with man in Christ. The cloud and fire, the *Shekinah,* came to dwell with us again in an especially tender, miraculous, and surprising way. "And the Word became flesh and dwelt among us, full of grace and truth; we have beheld his glory" (John 1:14). "Dwelt" in this context literally means "tabernacled," while *Shekinah* means "glory." Jesus is the new Tabernacle where the glory of God dwells.

Jesus connected his body to the new temple: "Destroy this temple, and in three days I will raise it up" (John 2:19). Joseph Cardinal Ratzinger (Pope Benedict XVI) explains that Jesus' body will take the place of the Old Testament Temple:

This is a prophecy of the Cross: he shows that the destruction of his earthly body will be at the same time the end of the Temple. With his Resurrection the new Temple will begin: the living body of Jesus Christ, which will now stand in the sight of God and be the place of all worship. Into this body he incorporates men. It is the tabernacle that no human hands have made, the place of true worship of God, which casts out the shadow and replaces it with reality.[3]

LIVING STONES

In a very real sense, everything true of the Old Testament Tabernacle is also true of us, individually and as the Church, because you and I are tabernacles, too. "By the grace of God, Christians also become temples of the Holy Spirit, living stones out of which the Church is built" (CCC 1197). Through us, the Church, God is literally present, "living" on the earth.

This glory-presence foreshadowed Eucharistic Adoration and Benediction today. As the incense rises before the Lord—in the presence of the people, singing *O Salutaris* and *Tantum Ergo*—the God of the Universe is with his sons and daughters in the monstrance (from the Latin word *monstrare,* meaning "to show"). Jesus Christ shows us his "face" and is truly and substantially present—Body, Blood, Soul, and Divinity—in the most Blessed Sacrament of the altar.

In the Old Testament, God dwelt in a portable tent, and it was the center of communal life for God's people and their place of worship. The Tabernacle was patterned after the one in heaven, and it foreshadowed the Church to come.

The Old Testament Law, the center of which was the Tabernacle, was humanity's tutor, training the Jews, and—through them—the world (us) to long for, seek, and recognize the fullness and maturity of faith and worship that would come through Christ and the Church he would establish: "Now before faith came, we were confined under the law, kept under restraint until faith should be revealed. So that the law was our custodian until Christ came, that we might be justified by faith" (Galatians 3:23-24).

Just before his ascension, Jesus left his apostles with instructions to wait in Jerusalem until the power of the Holy Spirit had come upon them (see Luke 24:49). He was referring to the descent of the Holy Spirit at Pentecost. The scriptural language is similar to the language the angel Gabriel used at the Annunciation, and it gives us a clue as to God's intent for the apostles and "for those who believe in [him] through their word" (John 17:20).

The presence of Mary among the apostles at Pentecost illustrates to us that she is the living connection between the earthly life of Christ— through the Incarnation—and the mystery of the Church as the body of Jesus (see Acts 1: 13-14; 1 Corinthians 12). Mary, the first living "temple," presented the infant Jesus to Simeon the priest to be offered back to God through her son's human nature. The Incarnation is the most extraordinary presence of God in the world.

In the New Testament, God dwells in a living tabernacle, the body of Christ, the Church, which is made of "living stones" (1 Peter 2:5). We are the Church! When we gather together in our parish churches to celebrate the sacraments, particularly the Eucharist, God is present in and through us. As the *Catechism* puts it:

> In its earthly state the Church needs places where the community can gather together. Our visible churches, holy places, are images of the holy city, the heavenly Jerusalem, toward which we are making our way on pilgrimage (CCC 1198).

What, then, is Christian worship, the "how" of the New Testament? It is built firmly on the foundation of the Old Testament.

LET'S REVIEW

The Tabernacle is able to concisely communicate our Faith because:

- God is always calling man to worship in his presence.

- God explains how to worship him properly, in a way that draws us into the closest possible relationship to him.

- God longs to make a home in us.

- God is completely consistent: New Testament worship and practice is built on the foundation of the Old Testament.

- In the Old Testament Law, God gave detailed instructions for whole-life liturgical worship centered around the Tabernacle.

- The Old Testament Tabernacle was a copy of the sanctuary in heaven and the prototype of the Church to come.

- New Testament worship should resemble both Old Testament and heavenly worship.

- Jesus is the new and final Tabernacle of worship. The Church is his body, built of "living stones."

- The only religious group that contains every piece of proper worship commanded by God is the Catholic Church.

INVITATION

In addition to equipping you to confidently share your faith with those you know and love, the goal of this book is for you to come to sense more deeply through the Tabernacle that Jesus is a living, breathing part of your life—if you allow him to be. Thomas à Kempis taught:

> Whatever be the affair, enter with Moses into the Tabernacle to ask advice of the Lord, you will sometimes hear the divine answer and return instructed in many things present and to come. For Moses always had recourse to the Tabernacle for the solution of doubts and questions, and fled to prayer for support in dangers and the evil deeds of men. So you also should take refuge in the secret chamber of your heart, begging earnestly for divine aid.[4]

Let us pray.

God Prompt – LOVE the Word ™

LISTEN: "And let them make me a sanctuary, that I may dwell in their midst" (Exodus 25:8).

OBSERVE: In what areas of your life do you most need God's presence, help, or instruction?

Have you invited him there? Explain.

In what specific areas might God want to work in your life through this book as you make room for him there?

What are your goals in reading this book?

What is the most significant statement or Scripture passage you read today? What does God want you to do in response?

VERBALIZE: Lord, the areas of my life that need you most are ...

My deepest desires about these areas are ...

From what I understand you to be saying so far about them, your will seems clear here ...

But not so clear here ...

 ENTRUST: *Lord, I believe it is your desire to tabernacle with me, to be present in my life and circumstances. Help me learn to make my heart a sanctuary in which you can be comfortable and fully present. I commit these challenges to you in the coming weeks and ask for direction in these areas. I believe. Help my unbelief.*

— Keeping Time with God —

*The Jewish Feasts Are Fulfilled
in the Sacred Liturgical Year*

The Easter Vigil when I was received into full communion with the Church was wondrous for me. I was in my thirties, and I remember thinking that I had never before properly celebrated this glorious season.

I had spent that entire Lent in quiet. I gave up coffee. I meditated on the sorrowful mysteries of the Rosary every day. I watched *The Passion of the Christ.* I did the Stations of the Cross. I attended every Liturgy of Holy Week.

I couldn't wait to receive my first Eucharist and become one in communion with all my new brothers and sisters. But I loved the agony of waiting, too, because I remembered my vehement prayer from many years ago, the prayer he was about to answer in a way I could have never anticipated: "Lord, I just want to be *closer* to you! Isn't there some way we can be closer?" Waiting made me long to be one with Jesus all the more.

At the Easter Vigil, I bawled like a baby through the entire Liturgy. The next morning, Easter Sunday, I went to Mass even though I had participated in the Vigil, just so I could celebrate Jesus' resurrection again, hear it proclaimed again, sing about it again, and say again, "He is risen *indeed!*" I was so excited that the Easter Season would last for *fifty days* until Pentecost!

I had lived through three decades of Easters without such an intensity of participation. Before being received into the Catholic Church, I do not think I had ever experienced what Easter was *really* all about. Although not with the same zeal as that first year, I still love getting into the "Lenten zone" each year. What makes all the difference for me? It is the Church's liturgical calendar. Whose great idea was the liturgical year? It was God's!

PROFESSING TIME'S SACREDNESS

God knows what we need. We need rest! It is written in natural law and preserved in the Ten Commandments that we give time to God. Rest is both spiritual and physical, so ignoring our inherent need for worship combined with rest is detrimental to our physical, emotional, and spiritual health. In addition to a physical structure, proper worship was meant to include an annual worship schedule, solemn ceremonies, and vivid rituals.

As a non-Catholic, the word "liturgy" was foreign to me, but I learned that it comes from the Greek word *leitourgia,* meaning "a work of the people." In its broadest sense, "liturgy" simply means "a ritual for public worship." It is important to note, though, that liturgy in the Old Testament denoted God's presence. Liturgy, then, is not about style or preference, but *presence.* Liturgy is God's way of sanctifying space and time. God gives us worship liturgy, so it is not according to self-expression, individual desire, or arbitrary wishes; we do not presume to invent or eliminate sacred liturgy for ourselves. Instead, liturgy is prayer most fully in God's presence, an attitude of orientation toward God, of listening, sensing, and receiving God as "holy other" in wonder and adoration.

SACRED *MOADIM*

Proper worship was centered around God's presence in the Tabernacle in a set liturgical schedule of hours, days, weeks, months, and years—known as *moadim* ("seasons")—that kept the people's minds and hearts looking upward to God in covenant and anticipating his covenant action in their everyday lives. In his *Summa Theologica,* St. Thomas Aquinas relates that time is an imperfection because it measures change, and God is unchangeable.[5] Sometimes it is said that time is God's way of stopping everything from happening at once. By ordaining their observance of this sacred schedule of holy, festive days centered around the Tabernacle, God was teaching his people that space and time were created for worship. Time is sacred, so it is not *mine* at all, but a gift in which I experience God as present. God called these festive days *his* "appointed feasts" (Leviticus 23:2).

Additionally, the seven major *moadim* were themselves based on sevens, which, as we see with the Sabbath, is the number associated with covenant and therefore also symbolic of completeness and divinity. The *moadim* were celebrated in two different periods corresponding to the two agricultural seasons. In Israel, there was a time of rain in the spring called the "former" or "early" rain and a time of rain in the fall called the "latter" rain. This division was related to the two appearances the Messiah was prophesied to make on the earth: "He will come to us as the showers, as the spring rains that water the earth" (Hosea 6:3).

Continuing the pattern in sevens, the seventh day was the Sabbath; seven Sabbaths were the week of Passover; seven weeks of seven Sabbaths were the Feast of Pentecost; the seventh month celebrated the Feasts of Trumpets, Atonement, and Tabernacles; the seventh year and the seventh seven of years were years of Jubilee. God uses time to "seven himself" in covenant to his people and creation. The Israelites' observance of the *moadim* united them to him in covenant time.

Unlike pagan religions, which thought of time as an endless cycle, the liturgical year communicated that time had a definite beginning and a definite end. The people were meant to learn through the Tabernacle and its schedule that God draws close to us in time and space. He is lord of our time, of *all* time and history. By his providence, all times and seasons are ordered. God invites us to live and work with him there. How exciting!

The world likes to marginalize the Christian as tangential to human history and anthropology. But God created time for man to worship in, and the Old Testament liturgical year, centered around the Tabernacle, provided the framework for the whole-life worship of his people that made them conscious of God's lordship over time and history.

The liturgical year lends itself to a sort of spiral timeline view, moving ever forward, upward, and toward the Day of Judgment. There are so many interesting things to learn about the ceremonies and rituals associated with each feast in the Jewish sacred calendar. There were other sacred times in the Old Testament liturgical year, but the major annual festivals were Passover, Unleavened Bread, First Fruits, Weeks, Trumpets, the Day of Atonement, and Booths (Tabernacles).

The Sabbath is the basis for all the other Old Testament feasts and the blueprint of Christians' Sunday worship. The Sabbath commemorated God's Creation of the heavens and the earth, in which the Garden of Eden was a large temple (like the Holy of Holies) and the human person was made for worship. The content and sevenfold covenantal structure of Genesis 1–3 is itself liturgical, with the seventh day occupying Creation's high point. If Eden represents a Holy of Holies in God's "temple" of creation, the implication is that humanity, created for the mysterious intimacy of this inner sanctuary, is best understood as "liturgical man." Living in the Holy of Holies, humanity is called to give worship to God in every thought, word, and deed. Through the Sabbath, and now our Sunday, we learn that we must remain close to God and "keep time" with him in our tabernacles. Now we will turn our attention to the pilgrimage feasts.

PILGRIMAGE FEASTS

The First Festival Octave, Passover

The three major Jewish feasts—Passover, Weeks, and Booths—were pilgrimage festivals, because once the people settled in the Promised Land, every able-bodied male was called back to Jerusalem three times a year to celebrate and offer sacrifices in worship at the Temple with his countrymen (see Exodus 34:23).

Biblical ceremonial law regulated liturgy and worship and commemorates the principle saving event for the people. In addition to one day a week, God's saving action in delivering his people from Egyptian slavery was so important that it required a whole week's observance. A sort of weeklong Sabbath and the first "holy week," the annual Feasts of Passover and Unleavened Bread reminded the people of God's special care for them in the Exodus.

Initially, God sent Moses to ask Pharaoh to let the Hebrew slaves go to Mount Sinai to worship him. Pharaoh refused. God warned Pharaoh through Moses that he would send plagues if Pharaoh did not relent and let his people go. The last, most devastating of those plagues was the death of every firstborn of both man and beast in the kingdom.

The original Passover story is told in Exodus 12 (both "exodus" and "Moses" mean "drawn out," or "leaving"). It was spring, March or early April. To protect them from the plague of the firstborn, God told the Hebrew people to kill a sacrificial spring lamb and splash its blood on their doorposts (see Exodus 12:13). The blood of the lamb was necessary because when the angel of death went through the Egyptian kingdom to administer the plague of death on every firstborn, he would "pass over" all the homes that had the sign of lamb's blood on the doorposts.

That same night, they were to roast the lamb and eat it with unleavened bread in what would become an annual Hebrew communal meal. They could not share it with anyone from a different household, with anyone who was "passing through," nor anyone who was not a circumcised Israelite (see Exodus 12:45-49), but every convert was an equal and was entitled to his share. Their bread had to be unleavened because they were in a hurry (see Exodus 12:11). God delivered them so swiftly and miraculously that first Passover, that they had no time to make preparations or wait for their bread to rise. Later, "leaven" (meaning to "sour" or "ferment") became symbolic of sin in the Bible, as if to convey that on our pilgrimage home to heaven, we have no time to allow sin to ferment and take over our lives.

Like the Sabbath, the Passover feast was meant to be observed forever. "This day shall be for you a memorial day, and you shall keep it as a feast to the LORD; throughout your generations you shall observe it as an ordinance for ever" (Exodus 12:14). The children of Israel were to keep the Passover and all the liturgical feasts as a perpetual covenant. For the Jewish people, feasts were forward-looking. The prophets understood the liturgical feasts to be typological of a new exodus, in which the Spirit would give a new law and the grace to live it (see Ezekiel 36). For the Jews, a "memorial" does not mean "to remember the past" in the way we recall something that happened previously in our lives. And it is not simply a remembrance of an important event that happened in Jewish history thousands of years before. When Jews celebrate the Passover, they "re-participate" in the Passover event in Egypt.

God's people kept the Passover feast all the way to Jesus' time, at which point he became the new Passover, the Paschal Lamb, in his person. We see in John 1:29 that John the Baptist calls Jesus the Lamb *(pasch)* of God who takes away the sin of the world. Jesus is the fulfillment of all those many years of Old Testament sacrificial lambs.

The Passover lamb's body and blood removed the judgment of physical death from the Hebrew people during the first Old Covenant Passover, and they commemorated that event throughout their history. Jesus, the Lamb of God, established a New Covenant and a new Passover that would remove our *eternal, spiritual* death sentence.

> Now as they were eating, Jesus took bread, and blessed, and broke it, and gave it to the disciples and said, "Take, eat; this is my body." And he took a cup, and when he had given thanks he gave it to them, saying, "Drink of it, all of you; for this is my blood of the covenant, which is poured out for many for the forgiveness of sins" (Matthew 26:26-28).

Jesus' words are an almost exact repeat of his teachings in John 6:

> Jesus said to them, "Truly, truly, I say to you, unless you eat the flesh of the Son of man and drink his blood, you have no life in you; he who eats my flesh and drinks my blood has eternal life, and I will raise him up at the last day. For my flesh is food indeed, and my blood is drink indeed. He who eats my flesh and drinks my blood abides in me, and I in him" (John 6:53-56).

Just as their ancestors had previously eaten the roasted lamb's body and marked their doorposts with its blood, the apostles were commanded to eat Jesus' Body and drink his Blood, and as often as they did, the effect of the covenant would be the forgiveness of sins (see Matthew 26:28). It was not by accident that Jesus instituted the Eucharist and was crucified as the sacrificial Lamb of God on the Jewish feasts of Unleavened Bread and Passover. Unlike the Passover lambs, whose blood caused the angel of death to "pass over" God's people, Jesus' Blood truly takes away the sin of the world, fulfilling these Old Covenant feasts in his own Body and Blood, so that they remain forever.

In a way similar to the Jewish people of the Old Testament, we consume the Lamb. His Blood is then applied to the "doorposts" of our hearts, saving us from the eternal consequences of sin. Oh, how this truth makes my heart soar! Keeping this new Passover feast—the Eucharist—draws the Lamb into our hearts to dwell. Jesus comes to tabernacle with us through the Eucharist we celebrate at Mass every Sunday and every Easter. Because of this, Sunday is often called a "little Easter."

The Old Testament Passover is fulfilled in Christ, who is our Passover. As St. Paul tells us in 1 Corinthians 5:7-8, "For Christ, our paschal lamb, has been sacrificed. Let us, therefore, celebrate the festival." This is important, because some Christians believe all feasts are legalistic and have been eliminated in the New Covenant. St. Paul taught and practiced otherwise. The Bible commands us to keep the feast. Catholics keep the New Covenant Passover feast—Easter. We do this daily and weekly at Mass and annually at Easter, along with our other liturgical celebrations.

Lord of the Seasons, the Feast of Weeks

I grew up living on a largely self-sufficient farm. Our orchards, vineyard, and enormous vegetable garden kept us busy and sweaty most of the year. My summers off from school were spent on those acres of land, stringing and breaking five-gallon buckets full of green beans in front of TV movies while my parents were at work. My mother spent hours canning and preserving hundreds of jars of corn, beans, tomatoes, pickles, squash, and peppers. Colorful quart jars of home-grown vegetables and fruit lined our cellar walls and nourished us all winter. For us, like many rural farmers, harvest time brought with it great celebration and fun.

During harvest time in the Old Testament, God instructed his people to keep him in mind as Harvest Giver through special festivals. They were to cease from work, gather at the Tabernacle, and present offerings of thanksgiving to him, the Lord of the Harvest. The Feast of Weeks was one such celebration, also known by a name more familiar to us: Pentecost. The term "weeks" represented seven weeks of seven days. That is forty-nine days, plus the one on which the feast began, equaling fifty. Therefore, Pentecost was approximately a two-month festival that got its name from the Greek word for "fifty." Pentecost formally began with the one-day Feast of First Fruits. The two feasts were quickly combined into one, however, so we will look at them together.

Leviticus 23:9-22 shows us that the Feasts of First Fruits and Pentecost were, together, a religious celebration of the grain harvest. Before the people could eat any of the grain of a new harvest, they were to bring a bundle to the Tabernacle in proportion to how much God had blessed them that year. The priest would "wave," or elevate, the offerings before God as a gift of thanksgiving (see Leviticus 23:11). The offering was a little like a thanksgiving tithe, right off the top, and it acknowledged the people's reliance on God's faithful provision of the harvest. It was also an expectation that God would provide the rest of the harvest as his continued blessing. Like the others, these feasts were to last forever (see Leviticus 23:14).

The Jews looked forward, anticipating the coming Messiah, or Christ. As Christians, we look back to his first coming; his public ministry; his passion, death, and resurrection; and his ascension into heaven. We also look forward to the Second Coming and the "day" the feasts will no longer be required, as time shall be no more. Christians keep the new law of the Holy Spirit—to love one another—which Jesus commanded (see Romans 13:8-10). This law includes the feasts that help us love and remember the sacred occasions upon which Christianity is built. They keep us "in time" with God in a similar way that the former liturgical feasts did for God's Chosen People.

The Birthday of the Church, First Fruits

As part of the Temple ceremony, at First Fruits, the priest would take some of the barley, lift it up, and wave it to God in the sight of all the people. One of the foundational doctrines of our Faith is the resurrection of Christ. This event was foreshadowed in the Feast of First Fruits. Not only did Jesus die on Passover, but he rose on the Feast of First Fruits. "And I, when I am lifted up from the earth, will draw all men to myself" (John 12:32). St. Paul connected the Resurrection to this feast when he said, "But in fact Christ has been raised from the dead, the first fruits of those who have fallen asleep" (1 Corinthians 15:20).

The Feast of Pentecost informally began with First Fruits, but while whole stalks of grain were waved before God in the Tabernacle at First Fruits, they were ground into flour and baked into loaves to offer to him with gifts of wine at Pentecost (see Leviticus 23:13-22). For the Jews, Pentecost also commemorated the giving of the Law on Mount Sinai, which later Jewish rabbis purport to have happened fifty days after the people left Egypt (see Exodus 19:1-2).

During these seven weeks, the Israelites prepared themselves to receive the Torah through purity rituals that helped rid them of the residue of slavery and that consecrated them as a holy nation ready to stand before God. Rabbis compare this event to a wedding between God and his Chosen People.

With this feast schedule context in mind, Jesus, as a faithful Jew, gave his disciples careful instructions immediately after his resurrection, telling them to "wait for the promise of the Father," the Holy Spirit:

> When the day of Pentecost had come, they were all together in one place. And suddenly a sound came from heaven like the rush of a mighty wind, and it filled all the house where they were sitting. And there appeared to them tongues as of fire, distributed and resting on

each one of them. And they were all filled with the Holy Spirit and began to speak in other tongues, as the Spirit gave them utterance (Acts 2:1-4).

Remember that in the Old Testament, the Feast of Pentecost actually began with the one-day Feast of First Fruits. St. Paul uses the term "first fruits" in 1 Corinthians 15:17-23 to refer to the resurrection of Christ as the "first fruits" from the dead, because the Old Testament Feast of First Fruits corresponds with the New Testament resurrection of Christ, the "first fruit" of the bodily resurrection. If he is the "first fruit," we are the fruit that follows. This is why we proclaim the following in the Nicene Creed every Sunday at Mass: "I believe in one, holy, catholic and apostolic Church. I confess one Baptism for the forgiveness of sins and I look forward to the resurrection of the dead and the life of the world to come."

Jesus also draws a connection between himself and a seed, saying the seed is somehow "glorified" by dying because in doing so, it produces a great harvest.

And Jesus answered them, "The hour has come for the Son of man to be glorified. Truly, truly, I say to you, unless a grain of wheat falls into the earth and dies, it remains alone; but if it dies, it bears much fruit" (John 12:23-24).

Pentecost is sometimes called the birthday of the Church, and the gift the Church received was the Holy Spirit, made possible by the death and resurrection of Christ. The disciples listened to Jesus' instructions and waited prayerfully after his ascension. And on a feast ripe with the promise of harvest and the remembrance of Sinai, the Holy Spirit fell upon them as a loud, visible, life-giving "power from on high" (Luke 24:49). That particular Pentecost was the day of first fruits of the Church, the beginning of the great harvest of souls that would become the new people of God, the new "bride," through the Holy Spirit. On that Pentecost, a new people of God was born of the spiritual fertility of the Third Person of the Trinity, as St. Jerome poetically wrote:

> There is Sinai, here Zion; there the trembling mountain, here the trembling house; there the flaming mountain, here the flaming tongues; there the noisy thunderings, here the sounds of many tongues; there the clangor of the rams horn, here the notes of the gospel-trumpet.

This Valley of Tears, the Feast of Booths

The final pilgrimage feast, the Feast of Booths, also called the Feast of Tabernacles, reminds us that God always provides for us while we are on this pilgrimage of wandering in the wilderness on our way to the Promised Land. The Hail Holy Queen prayer expresses this wandering, lost feeling beautifully: "To thee do we send up our sighs, mourning and weeping in this valley of tears."

In the Feast of Tabernacles, God instructed the people to make themselves lean-tos out of branches and to camp outside in them for a week in remembrance of their journey through the wilderness (see Leviticus 23:39-42). The feast kept the people looking toward the eternal tabernacle while they wandered through the wilderness of life to the "motherland," heaven.

YOU REAP WHAT YOU SOW

As you can see, the Bible has quite a lot to say about planting and harvesting, but as we close out this chapter, we are going to look at a brief set of principles conveniently contained in a specific passage. The people of biblical times lived much closer to the land and seasons than we do. They understood these principles like they knew how to breathe. It may seem simplistic, but my mama always warned me with a lesson from the Bible growing up, and I never forgot it. The passage is so important that I am including it here in its entirety. We are going to unpack the whole thing together:

> Do not be deceived; God is not mocked, for whatever a man sows, that he will also reap. For he who sows to his own flesh will from the flesh reap corruption; but he who sows to the Spirit will from the Spirit reap eternal life. And let us not grow weary in well-doing, for in due season we shall reap, if we do not lose heart (Galatians 6:7-9).

Consider getting some colored pencils, pens, or highlighters to make notes in your Bible. In the passage from Galatians, underline, "Do not be deceived; God is not mocked" (Galatians 6:7). This is as strong a warning as one sees in the Bible. Scripture warns us not to fool ourselves. God's justice demands order, and that order is built into the cosmos. You *will* reap what you sow.

In a different color, draw a circle around, "Whatever a man sows, that he will also reap" (Galatians 6:7). At Creation, God established that everything would produce "according to its kind" (Genesis 1:11). We understand this naturally, but have you considered that it is true *spiritually* as well? Just as one cannot sow carrots and produce pumpkins or breed goats and get trout, so, too, one cannot sow sin and produce peace. We cannot sow antagonism and produce unity. We cannot sow lies and produce truth. We cannot sow selfishness and produce love. You will reap *what* you sow.

Choose another color and draw a box around, "He who sows to the Spirit will from the Spirit reap" (Galatians 6:8). If we plant, we will harvest. We cannot harvest savings if we do not plant economy. If we do not plant disciplined, persistent, informed prayers, our lives will not produce holiness, peace, or spiritual fruit in ourselves or others. You will reap *if* you sow.

In a fourth color, draw an arrow pointing to "in due season" (Galatians 6:9). According to Genesis 8:22, "While the earth remains, seedtime and harvest, cold and heat, summer and winter, day and night, shall not cease." The harvest never comes immediately after planting, for while the earth abides, "there is a season, and a time for every matter under heaven" (Ecclesiastes 3:1). No harvest is produced immediately. What you sow now will surely take time to grow, "first the blade, then the ear, then the full grain in the ear" (Mark 4:28). But it will grow. We must not lose heart, grow discouraged, or quit. You reap *after* you sow, sometimes long after.

In a light color, highlight the words *flesh* and *corruption, Spirit* and *eternal life.* Seeds of the flesh tend toward complete rot; seeds of the Spirit tend toward abundant life. A single seed reaps a much bigger harvest. This principle is all over Scripture. "For they sow the wind, and they shall reap the whirlwind" (Hosea 8:7). You reap *more than* what you sow.

So the principles of harvest are:

- You reap *what* you sow.
- You reap what you sow *in kind.*
- You reap *if* you sow.
- You reap *after* you sow.
- You reap *more than* you sow.

God's activity in time and history constantly moves between the two poles of natural creation and supernatural grace and redemption. While nature produces what we naturally sow, namely death and sin, the Spirit produces redemption and life through supernatural grace.

We see this particularly in the differences between the feasts of the Old Testament and those of the New Testament. The Old Testament pilgrimage feasts and our later Christian feasts serve as annual reminders that our Creator still works miracles, granting his Spirit to those called to be the first fruits of his exponential spiritual harvest, empowering them to carry out his work throughout history and the world. Through our liturgical celebrations, God calls us to a more deliberate participation in and remembrance of his action in our lives and the world. But we must first be faithful to sow what is good and give back to God.

Many people spend their income first on themselves and their families and then give to charity and the Church some part of what is left over. For those, the Bible is vocal that the law of sowing and reaping will not be circumvented:

> You have looked for much, and lo, it came to little; and when you brought it home, I blew it away. Why? says the LORD of hosts. Because of my house that lies in ruins, while you busy yourselves each with his own house (Haggai 1:9).

The lessons of the liturgical feasts suggest, instead, that the first and best portion is due to God and that the concern of his kingdom is the first duty of our income. This is true because the harvest of my salary is first and foremost *God's* activity, not of my own power. Without the breath he gives me daily, I could not work, build, or earn anything at all.

SPIRAL STAIRWAY TO HEAVEN, A YEAR OF CELEBRATIONS

Catholics experience the passing of seasons, days, and hours as repeating cycles of meditations on the sacred mysteries of Christ. Like the Israelites, Catholics relive the action of God in history every year through the liturgical calendar, which is centered around the parish in a whole-life way. We re-present the Gospel with the whole community of God's people from Christ's birth and public ministry to his passion, death, resurrection, and ascension.

The Old Testament liturgical schedule was something of a repeating pattern, or template, for all religious history and time. God must have wanted his people to be celebrating all the time, because there were more feasts throughout the year that helped them balance work and play. The feasts had an immediate agricultural significance, and they also commemorated national events of the Israelites. Through the Church, we see that this is still true. God fulfilled and carried forward the old feasts and festivals into the Church and time through Christ so that they remained perpetual, as he commanded all those millennia ago. We know that keeping Christian feasts is really a participation of the heavenly celebration occurring as we speak, in anticipation of the final celebration of Christ's union with the Church at the Wedding Feast of the Lamb at the end of history. I find that a comforting meditation.

The Liturgy is the official divine worship of the Church (see CCC 1163–1171). Just as God commanded, it takes place within an annual liturgical calendar, is centered in the parish, and is a "whole-life" endeavor that helps us balance work and rest.

The overarching point of this schedule is that we both remember salvation past and anticipate salvation future. Therefore, the liturgical calendar is not just a bunch of random days that require us to go to Mass, give us days off, and offer fun family traditions and happy songs. No one "makes" or "invents" liturgical worship.

The Old Testament liturgical schedule was established by God and centered around the Tabernacle, foreshadowing our Church's liturgical year. The Church's feast days are days of obligation, like those of the Old Testament, and include rest, worship, offerings, and gathering of God's people. Isn't it marvelous that through the holy days of the Church, especially Sundays, we participate in the heavenly celebration occurring right now? At Mass, especially, we connect with the angels and the saints who are already celebrating in heaven.

By keeping time with God through the liturgical year, the Church on earth shows it is united with the liturgy of heaven. How wonderful that our liturgical calendar points us to heaven, in which we will ultimately worship in communion forever with Jesus. Amen! It was this sense of connectedness to past, present, and future saints that made my first Easter as a Catholic so meaningful to me.

> From the time of the Mosaic law, the People of God have observed fixed feasts, beginning with Passover, to commemorate the astonishing actions of the Savior God, to give him thanks for them, to perpetuate their remembrance, and to teach new generations to conform their conduct to them. In the age of the Church, between the Passover of Christ already accomplished once for all, and its consummation in the kingdom of God, the liturgy celebrated on fixed days bears the imprint of the newness of the mystery of Christ (CCC 1164).

LET'S REVIEW

The Catholic Church has a liturgical year because:

- The Old Testament liturgical schedule was established by God and centered around the Tabernacle, foreshadowing our Church's liturgical year.

- Through the Old Testament Sabbath, God indicated his perpetual desire that man rest and worship in imitation of his own Sabbath rest and look forward to our final, heavenly rest.

- The Church's feast days are days of obligation, like those of the Old Testament, that include rest, worship, offerings, and gathering of God's people.

- Through our holy days, especially Sunday and Easter, we participate in the heavenly liturgy and communion feast.

- At Mass, we connect with the angels and the saints who are already celebrating in heaven.

- Our liturgical calendar points us to heaven, in which we will ultimately worship in communion forever with Jesus.

- We cannot live in the closest possible relationship with God if our time is not centered and ordered in him and his Church.

INVITATION

Like the Israelites in the Old Testament, Catholics relive the action of God in history every year through the liturgical year. We "re-present" the Gospel from Christ's incarnation and birth, to his passion, ascension, and reign. In spring, he enters the world in Mary's immaculate womb; in winter, he is born, circumcised, and named. He is raised in the Holy Family and meets his cousin John. He goes into the desert—and we go with him—during Lent. We follow him through his passion, which is soon vanquished by his resurrection, ascension, and Pentecost. Now he reigns, and we await his second coming as we prepare to celebrate his first coming again. Then the cycle begins again, like a wheel that has been spinning for two millennia. When we participate in this spiral of remembrance and anticipation by celebrating the feasts of the Church, God lives intimately in time and history with us. Let us pray.

God Prompt – LOVE the Word™

LISTEN: "You shall keep my sabbaths, for this is a sign between me and you" (Exodus 31:13).

OBSERVE: What is the most significant statement or Scripture passage you read in this chapter?

Do you desire refreshing from the Lord? In what area of your life do you need his rest?

How has God spoken to you in this chapter about how you treat Sundays and other holy days?

What steps can you take to make Sunday a more holy day, a day of rest, for yourself and your family?

VERBALIZE: Lord, you have shown me that my primary challenge about Sunday obligation is ...

Lord, I sense you calling me to a more restful, reverent Sunday. In all honesty, I am probably experiencing very little mental, emotional, and spiritual rest because I rest and worship so little on Sundays. One way I commit to making my Sundays more restful and worshipful is by ...

 ENTRUST: *Lord, I believe it is your desire to be present with us in all of our work and rest and in all of our days, weeks, and years. Help us make your holy days more holy, especially by being faithful in gathering at church and giving our souls a Sunday. We commit these feasts more carefully to you, and we thank you for the gift of rest!*

A Kingdom of Priests

The Levitical Priesthood Is
Fulfilled in the Catholic Priesthood

Through the very existence of the Tabernacle, God communicated his desire for whole-life worship, in which he could be fully at home with his people. But it had to be a special kind of worship, something wholly "other." Proper worship for the people of God would be liturgical, and all the rites, ceremonies, and sacrifices offered on their behalf would require a special representative— the priest.

Descriptions of the vestments and ordination and consecration rites of the first priests are recorded in Leviticus 8, with parallel passages in Exodus 28 and 29. Together they give us a thorough account of the sacred ceremony that set these priests wholly apart for God's service.

THE OLD TESTAMENT PRIESTHOOD

Aaron was chosen by God to be high priest and his sons as priests under him. God directed that Moses should ordain them, anointing them with precious, fragrant oil poured from a ram's horn, and clothing them with beautiful, elaborate vestments he personally specified for their "glory" and "beauty" (Exodus 28:2).

When Jesus reached the age of thirty—the age when one's priestly service could begin—he was formally "set apart" for his work, not as the levitical priests by anointing with symbolic oil, but by the anointing of the Holy Spirit at his baptism. He is the *Messiah* (or *Christ*), meaning the "anointed one."

As were all the materials and facilities in the Tabernacle, priestly vestments were fashioned from offerings by the people from the spoils of Egypt and made holy by special consecration to God's service. Next to the flesh, every priest wore a set of linen trousers for modesty's sake. Much like a religious habit, these would have been decidedly countercultural to the sexually preoccupied worship of Israel's neighbors. Over this was a white, seamlessly woven linen shirt, and a "girdle" or belt. The rest of the vestments belonged to the Aaronic high priest alone.

Over the shirt, the high priest's robe was a flowing garment of blue, probably seamless, reinforced at the neck, and decorated at the hem with a row of alternating miniature gold bells and multi-colored pomegranates. The bells tinkled as the priest moved about the Tabernacle sanctuary, letting the people know he had not died of sacrilege while serving on their behalf (see Exodus 28:35). The pomegranate was an ancient symbol of love and fruitfulness.

Over the robe, he wore the "ephod"—a long jacket of gold, scarlet, purple, and blue, embroidered after the pattern and colors of the veil. These are repeating colors of a touching significance throughout the Tabernacle that we will explore in a later chapter. The two linen sections of the ephod covered the priest's back and chest, with an opening for his head, seams at the shoulders, and a wide band around the waist that was of one piece with the ephod. At the shoulders were onyx stones, engraved with the names of each of the six tribes and fastened with filigreed braids of gold chain, depicting how the priesthood shouldered responsibility for the people and carried their sins and sorrows to God.

The breastplate of judgment was a strip of linen, folded into a small pouch that hung from the priest's neck and was emblazoned with distinctive gemstones: four rows of three different stones with the name of a tribe on each. The pouch contained two mysterious "stones of decision," called *Urim* and *Thummim*. Altogether, the breastplate illustrated how the priest carried the people and his decision making on their behalf on his heart before God. The Jewish historian Josephus says the gems in the breastplate revealed God's special presence with his people in battles:

> God declared beforehand, by those twelve stones which the high priest bare on his breast, and which were inserted into his breastplate, when they should be victorious in battle; for so great a splendor shone forth from them before the army began to march, that all the people were sensible of God's being present for their assistance.[6]

No mention is made of shoes or sandals; the priests officiated in bare feet in echo of God's command to Moses at the burning bush: "Put off your shoes from your feet, for the place on which you are standing is holy ground" (Exodus 3:5).

This priesthood, under God's instruction, depicts modesty, reverence, purity, and innocence, all typified by whiteness. The splendor of their intercessory office was displayed in the rich colors and precious jewels that relieved the whiteness. God's love and mercy for his people burned in the names of the people on the breastplate that heaved with every throb of the high priest's heart. His responsibility for them was confessed by the same names upon his shoulders, where their governance is said to have pressed like a load (see Isaiah 9:6).

To cap off the entire elaborate ensemble, the priest wore a ceremonial headdress, similar to a bishop's mitre. Made of white linen, it was secured in place at the seat of the priest's intelligence, his forehead, with a gold plate engraved with the stamp of God's absolute declaration: *Holiness to the LORD.*

Adam as Priest

When we think of the Old Testament priesthood, the previous description is usually what we mean. But priesthood goes back all the way to Adam. The Israelites understood all of creation to be a macro-temple, as is illustrated in the wisdom literature, which consistently describes Creation this way: "Who determined its measurements ... Or who stretched the line upon it? On what were its bases sunk, or who laid its cornerstone?" (Job 38:5-6).

As God created the cosmos in six days and consecrated and blessed it in covenant on the seventh, as the Tabernacle was consecrated in seven days, so, too, Solomon built the Temple in seven years and seven months. During a seven-day liturgy—where he offered seven petitions—he blessed and consecrated the Temple (see 1 Kings 5–9), illustrating that he also understood the Temple to be a micro-cosmos. Likewise, as the Tree of Life was located in the Garden, the menorah located in the Tabernacle and Temple was considered a stylized tree of life (see Exodus 25:31-40).

The "sanctuary" of the cosmos at Creation was understood to be the Garden of Eden. In Genesis 3:8, the language used to describe God as "walking in the garden" in the cool of the day is the same Hebrew word used in 2 Samuel 7:6-7 to describe God's presence moving about the Tabernacle in the wilderness. Similarly, there were cherubim stationed east of the Garden to guard its entrance (see Genesis 3:24). The entrance to the Tabernacle and the Temple faced east. The cherubim guarded the Ark of the Covenant in the Tabernacle, on the veil and the mercy seat. And two cherubim guarded the inner sanctuary of the Temple (see 1 Kings 6:23-28).

Every temple has a sanctuary; every sanctuary has a high priest to minister in it; and every high priest is "appointed to offer gifts and sacrifices" (Hebrews 8:3). The high priest in the Garden of Eden was Adam, who was given the duty to "till" and "keep" the garden, meaning "to serve" and "to guard." Later on in Scripture, whenever these words are used together, they always describe the duties of the priesthood in ministering in the Tabernacle and Temple (see Numbers 3:7-8, 8:26; Ezekiel 44:16).

Throughout the Torah and Jewish writings, Adam is depicted in stylized literary parallel as the high priest of humanity.[7] Adam was meant to fulfill the duties of a priest, to work in the sanctuary and offer sacrifice: he must "keep the charge" or guard the Garden from Satan, sin, and death, as was his sacrificial, priestly duty. Because all of humanity was "in" Adam and Eve, all of humanity fell with them (see CCC 404). Jesus, the new Adam in the spiritual order, offered the gift and sacrifice of himself for his bride, the Church, to save her from Satan, sin, and death (see 1 Corinthians 15:45).

Levitical Priesthood

From Adam, the priesthood passed through the family. When God spared the Jewish firstborn during the Plague of the Firstborn in Egypt, he "acquired" them and designated them for the special role of priest (see Exodus 13:1-2). Priesthood passed through the family in the firstborn son until Exodus 32 at the incident of the gold calf, where the pantheistic Egyptian ways were shown to be deeply entrenched in God's infant people, the Israelites. The Egyptians worshiped the cow and bull, and the bull was a widespread symbol for Baal worship in Canaan. Worship of these gods of wealth, fertility, and power involved sacrifice, a communion meal, and orgiastic sexual worship as the words "rose up to play" indicate (Exodus 32:6).

Moses received the gift of the Law on Mount Sinai as the people broke it at the foot of the mountain by making and worshiping a golden calf. God warned Moses of their idolatry, and Moses descended and broke the tablets of stone at its base in anger, demanding, "Who is on the LORD's side? Come to me" (Exodus 32:26). When the Levite tribes stepped forward to obey Moses' command to eliminate the idolaters, he proclaimed, "Today you have ordained yourselves for the service of the LORD" (Exodus 32:29). And a change in the priesthood occurred.

From that point forward, because they alone chose him, the Levites were set aside for God's service. God told Moses, "For they are wholly given to me from among the people of Israel; instead of all that open the womb, the firstborn of all the people of Israel, I have taken them for myself" (Numbers 8:16). In particular, Aaron and his sons and descendants, also Levites, would be the high priests, those who would offer sacrifices and serve the sanctuary. Numerous laws for animal sacrifice were commanded and recorded in the book of Leviticus. Morning and evening, they sacrificed to remind them and cleanse them of their idolatrous ways. Once a year, on the Day of Atonement, Aaron and those in the priestly line after him would sacrifice cattle as penance and atonement for Aaron's sin at the notorious golden calf incident.

THE RESURRECTION OF THE DEAD STICK

Probably the most serious argument non-Catholics pose against the Catholic Faith concerns its ministerial priesthood. Martin Luther had a problem with the institutional priesthood and worked to undermine it, because everything "Catholic" proceeds from it. As a Protestant, I grew up under the teaching that the priesthood was unnecessary. And yet the entire Old Testament testifies that God's people and their whole-life worship could never be legitimately separated from the priesthood. To divide the priesthood from Tabernacle or Temple worship would have been blasphemous, as the ghastly Great Apostasy of Israel was considered forever after it occurred. Additionally, Scripture says that because the law changed, the institutional priesthood was necessarily *changed,* not eliminated (see Ezekiel 44; Hebrews 7:12).

From Adam, Cain, and Abel onward, it became evident that the priesthood is part of the natural law. The perpetual institutional priesthood was also God's idea, fulfilled, dead, and obsolete in Jesus, our New Covenant, but resurrected in the Church through him much like Aaron's dead stick in the Holy of Holies.

In the Old Testament, those who murmured against the priesthood often died or were stricken with disease and other catastrophes. The consequence of this cycle of dissension and correction was division, a level of uncertainty among the people about whether Moses and Aaron had truly been divinely appointed. God was happy to clear up the controversy. To satisfy the issue of legitimate authority,

God, through Moses, publicly affirmed his institutional priesthood through the resurrection of the dead stick.

Jesus is the true Priest, fulfillment of the firstborn Adam, Melchizedek, Aaron, and the whole history of the levitical priesthood. He "mediates" a "better" covenant, which is "enacted on better promises" (Hebrews 8:6). The "better promises" are those of eternal life in his Body and Blood, because "the sacrifice of Christ and the sacrifice of the Eucharist *are one single sacrifice*" (CCC 1367). The *Catechism* goes on to state:

> The redemptive sacrifice of Christ is unique, accomplished once for all; yet it is made present in the Eucharistic sacrifice of the Church. The same is true of the one priesthood of Christ; it is made present through the ministerial priesthood without diminishing the uniqueness of Christ's priesthood: "Only Christ is the true priest, the others being only his ministers"[8] (CCC 1545).

In my own efforts at evangelization in the South, I have found that nothing irritates fundamentalist Christians like the priesthood. The priest is usually a person's first direct exposure to Church hierarchy, and let's face it, authority rubs us all the wrong way when it does not conform to what we think or want.

I can say so because, as I will share in more detail later, my whole spiritual education at God's hands has been on the issue of authority, and it was the number one issue that propelled me into the Catholic Church. I emerged from childhood with profound "father wounds" that provoked a sometimes violent rebellion against authority. My dad was angry, dominating, and controlling, so I became militantly feminist, striving for supremacy and determined no one would ever force me to do anything I didn't want to do ever again.

You can probably imagine how easy and joyful it was to be my father, my husband, my boss. Cough, cough. You can also understand, then, that I had real suspicions about church authority as well. When I was a twenty-something Baptist church leader, a dispute arose in our church against our pastor. It was nothing more than a personality conflict, really, but I chose a side and had all sorts of opinions that seemed completely righteous and just. After all, I could prove every one of those opinions with a Bible verse.

The problem was, God contradicted my opinions with his Word in *lectio divina,* and he used the Israelites' rebellion against the priesthood in Numbers 16–17 to do it. We have already seen the Israelites attack against the priesthood and how God affirmed through Aaron's rod the authority he had given his priests. The Lord took a similar approach with me when, as a young Baptist leader, I prayed about a high-handed pastor I disagreed with: "Who does he think he is? We are all a 'kingdom of priests!'" Our Protestant brothers and sisters place great stress on the "priesthood of all believers," which in effect means that no Christian is really a priest or that every man is "priest" in his own home and is responsible to conduct family prayers and biblical instruction.

But there is another attack on the institutional priesthood in the Bible that I believe is particularly instructive for our day and time. I think because of fear of my own father's authority and my respect for the Bible, I never went full-out in rebellion against that first pastor. But I think I would have eventually, in the most lady-like way, of course, had I stayed in my denomination. As a woman with a real call from God and a flourishing ministry teaching the Bible, I was "shushed" and publicly undermined by several men until a pastor, whom I respect dearly to this day, spiritually fathered me and lifted me up. I grew sick of the institutional condescension, so I understand the injustice of patriarchy as the term is usually used today.

But I implore you: For the sake of your soul and your true God-given spiritual influence and importance, please do not undermine God's authority in the Church, even in a behind-the-scenes, quiet way. We can and must work for justice, but we must do so within the parameters God gives us in his Word. What do I mean?

DEACONESSES, PROPHETESSES, PRIESTESSES … OH, MY

Recently, I read an article in which a Catholic laywoman lamented the injustice of the lack of "-esses" in the Catholic Church—that is, deaconesses, prophetesses, and priestesses. I confess I shuddered at the mental image her sentiment provoked, because a proper understanding of biblical patriarchy is unequivocally vital to relating to God, who reveals and expresses himself to humanity in terms of fatherhood and sonship. This is not, of course, the oppressive cultural "patriarchy" denounced by any healthy sense of justice; rather, it is a transcendent religious patriarchy that expresses who God is and how he wants us to relate to him. God is Giver; humanity receives from him. So, whether male or female, every human person is "feminine" in relation to God. Female priests (or "priestesses") are impossible, as this would usurp the most fundamental expression of who God is and how he relates to us.

Throughout history, priestesses were common in most pagan religions. In addition, these religions typically included temple prostitution and perverse sexual rituals that subjugated women in order to express or worship fertility. But elevation of fertility ignores the inherent complementary dependence on masculinity: to give life, a woman must receive a man's seed. She has no life-generating power of her own. Religious patriarchy, however distorted by human weakness, expresses the transcendence of God as ultimate Source and Giver. Strong biblical affirmation of religious patriarchy is due in part to correcting pagan religious views and practices, and the first such affirmation occurs in relation to the Tabernacle.

MIRIAM'S MISTAKE

Remember the older sister who placed the infant Moses in the basket and sent him floating toward Pharaoh's daughter on the Nile River? Her name was Miriam, and she was a Hebrew prophetess. In a display of the familiar music and dance prominent in Egyptian worship, where priestesses accompanied ceremonial dances and rituals with musical instruments, Miriam led Israelite worship after the people's rescue at the parting of the Red Sea (see Exodus 15:20). While they were not priestesses themselves, the wives of Egyptian priests often occupied these elevated singing, dancing, and musician roles in pagan temple worship, with instruments such as harps, tambourines, and sistras. As a prophetess, Miriam seems to have enjoyed a similar influential status in the Israelite camp. She spoke authoritatively from God and is listed in the Bible along with her brothers, Moses and Aaron (see Micah 6:4). With them, she occupied the highest role of leadership in Israel.

Neither she nor Aaron was ever Moses' equal in intimacy or authority with God, and that fact evidently rankled Miriam, who is listed first and received the full correction of God, implying that she was the instigator, when, not long into their Exodus to the Promised Land, Miriam and Aaron "spoke against Moses" about an Ethiopian woman Moses married (see Numbers 12).[9] Just as the lay priesthood rose up against Moses and Aaron and claimed equal authority, Miriam was not content with her privileged position either. In pride, she asserted a nonexistent "equal right" to the priesthood: "Has the LORD indeed spoken only though Moses? Has he not spoken through us also?" The verse ends ominously with the words, "And the LORD heard it" (Numbers 12:2).

"Suddenly," God descended in the cloud and called Miriam and Aaron forward like a parent: "Come out ... to the tent of meeting!" (Numbers 12:4). God pronounced his prerogative to select and to speak to whomever and however he chooses, and Miriam's judgment is recorded in dramatic poetry. When God withdrew in the cloud, Miriam was found with leprosy and formally expelled from the camp for seven days as unclean, even after her horrified brothers interceded on her behalf. Despite the shame of this event, Miriam remained in high regard throughout Jewish history.

Consistently throughout Scripture, rebellion against the priesthood creates a cycle of dissension (where the name "Protest-ant" comes from), division, and correction.

OUTWARD TO INWARD, AND UPWARD SPIRAL

Miriam's punishment, and other difficult Old Testament punishments, usually cause people to question why God seems so exacting in the Old Testament, where he ordered the total annihilation of entire cities, nations, people groups, and civilizations—men, women, children, property, and animals. They have trouble reconciling the Old Testament God with a tender, forgiveness-teaching Jesus; they may think the Old and New Testaments are at odds with one another.

The Bible, and salvation history contained therein, however, is laid out a little like an onion metaphor—you peel the layers from the outside in. Old Testament scholars tell us that such difficult punishments are examples of moral typology. God is probing and correcting the literal, visible, outward behavior of his infant people in the Old Testament. He is very strict, and the punishments are quick and sure, and even seem harsh at times. But the Old Testament lessons are those of children. God's Old Testament people came from the polytheism of Egypt, had no idea what worshiping one God meant, and did not have the indwelling power of the Holy Spirit to help them recognize or live up to the deeper need for grace. They were spiritual children. With children, boundaries must be very tight and the consequences quick and obvious; this is to ensure their safety and to prepare them to think and work more deeply when their development is ready for it.

In the same way, the Church teaches that God provided outward behaviors and boundaries through the Law that would keep his Old Testament children safe and teach them to properly worship the One True God, until he could lead them to the coming of the Messiah. At that point, he could move to deeper truths—inward behaviors—with a truly upward, heavenly momentum. Because the outward man had been tutored throughout Old Testament history, God could begin probing and correcting the spiritual, invisible, inward behavior of his more mature New Testament people at the proper time.

When God's people had matured and developed enough through history to handle deeper truths, he was faithful to reveal the fullness of himself through Christ, and the deeper, spiritual reality that he *is*. The spiritual depth of truth, reality, and life are the standard to which we are called by grace: "You shall be holy, for I am holy" (1 Peter 1:16). By grace, we can be holy. We can attain, experience, and communicate grace—the life of God himself that he longs to share with us. Incredible!

The principle is: outward to inward. The Old Testament addressed the outside. Outward concerns behavior. The New Testament addresses the interior soul as well as the outward behavior. Inward includes our interior perceptions and beliefs, the real motivations underneath our outward behaviors. Just like God corrected Miriam and the Israelite laity when they rebelled against God's authority, the Holy Spirit begins our spiritual formation by telling us the truth through Scripture about our outward behaviors and rebellion and then moves steadily more interiorly so he can bring us to our truest fulfillment.

SPIRITUAL PATRIARCHY AND MATRIARCHY

Recently, I was a speaker on a diverse panel of formidable women at Notre Dame University. We were discussing how to get beyond "liturgical cupcakes" in Catholic women's writing. Because one of my ministry maxims is, "Bible study spinach that tastes like cake," I probably felt more "cupcake-ey" and out-of-place than the others on the panel did. Right out of the chute, the discussion and questions from the audience took a heated turn to patriarchy in the Church. My heart sank, because I knew that with so many on the panel and only an hour, I would never be able to share more than this awkwardly received sentence about God and biblical patriarchy: namely, that God loves patriarchy because it images him, but it is a religious rather than a cultural patriarchy.

Edith Stein (St. Teresa Benedicta of the Cross), a Catholic feminist and philosopher killed by the Nazis at Auschwitz, spoke on the extraordinary capability and necessity of women in every realm of society and the Church: "We must consider as closed the historical epoch which made an absolute differentiation between the duties of the sexes, i.e., that woman should assume the domestic duties and man the struggle for a livelihood."[10] She conceded, though, that there is one essential difference that still exists in reality:

> Christ came to earth as the *Son* of Man. The first creature on earth fashioned in an unrivaled sense as God's image was therefore a man; that seems to indicate to me that he wished to institute only men as his official representatives on earth. Yet, he bound himself so intimately to *one* woman as no other on earth: He formed her so closely after his own image as no other human being before or after; he gave her a place in the Church for all eternity such as has been given to no other human being. And just so, he has called women in all times to the most intimate union with him.[11]

This is an important distinction, especially in our day of secular humanism, where the only authority is the individual, and feminism is working hard to erase the religious patriarchy that images God and was prescribed by him. An exclusively male priesthood does not detract from femininity but guards it. Pope Francis has said, "Women in the Church must be valued, not 'clericalized.' Whoever thinks of women as cardinals suffers a bit from clericalism."[12]

The belief that we must allow women to become priests to acknowledge or affirm their dignity is a clear misunderstanding of human dignity and the role of clergy *and* women. But maybe more important than the maxim "male priesthood because Jesus was a man" is the reality that motherhood is the natural feminine complement to priesthood. Priesthood is reserved to men as motherhood is reserved to women. Mary, as the new Miriam, restores this incontrovertible divine order in her person, instituting "a once and for all order of salvation in which the union of Mother and Child stands at the center."[13]

Bishop Fulton Sheen explains:

> Most of us love a non-self, or something extrinsic and apart from our inner life; but a mother's love during the time she is a flesh-and-blood ciborium is not for a non-self, but for one that is her very self, a perfect example of charity and love which hardly perceives a separation. Motherhood then becomes a kind pf priesthood. She brings God to man by preparing the flesh in which the soul will be implanted; she brings man to God in offering the child back again to the Creator ... she is nature's constant challenge to death, the bearer of cosmic plenitude, the herald of eternal realities, God's great cooperator.[14]

Everything must be done in order and according to one's role (see 1 Corinthians 14:40). Angels operate in hierarchy, and nature operates in hierarchy.

A BETTER PRIESTHOOD

Like everything else about the Old Testament Law, the institutional priesthood was a perpetual statute that could never be usurped or eliminated (see Exodus 29:9). For the priesthood to remain forever, it had to be "changed" into something "better" (see Hebrews 7:12, 19). The Old Testament Law brought nothing to perfection because it communicated no interior sanctity and it gave no power to do the good which it commanded. The introduction of grace through Christ is what makes the New Covenant "better." The book of Hebrews uses the term "better" ten times to describe the New Covenant.

The fact that the Church is the body of Christ on earth, his hands and feet, necessitates a New Testament institutional priesthood. What Jesus does in eternity, the Church does in time and history. What Jesus fulfills in himself, he also brings forward into New Testament history through the Church. St. Cyprian, writing around the year 250, said there is but "one altar and the one priesthood."[15]

The Catholic priesthood is the antitype of the resurrected almond branch, a living and fruitful priesthood instituted and invested with the grace of Christ himself and carried forward into his mystical body on earth. The grace conferred through the sacraments of the New Testament priesthood brings about perfection and brings us "near to God" (Hebrews 7:19). This priesthood is signified by the oath of the eternal Word of God made flesh, Jesus, who by his eternity can never be recanted (see Hebrews 7:20-28). The presence of Christ's sacred humanity in heaven is itself a perpetual pleading on our behalf. Our names are better written in his sacred wounds than the names of the twelve tribes on the gems of Aaron's breastplate, and his heart's desire for our salvation is always before God (see Romans 8:34).

Where the Old Testament sacrifices could not convey grace and elevate the people to holiness, the sacrifice of Christ that the priest offers on the altar—"through him, with him, and in him"—imparts eternal life according to the promise of Christ (see John 6:53-57). The Catholic priest serves the true sanctuary (see Hebrews 3:5-6), the living tabernacle of the Church in Christ's body. Where the Old Testament priesthood served the Law, the New Testament priesthood serves the Gospel.

> The ministerial priesthood is at the service of the common priesthood. It is directed at the unfolding of the baptismal grace of all Christians. The ministerial priesthood is a *means* by which Christ unceasingly builds up and leads his Church (CCC 1547).

OLD TESTAMENT HIERARCHY

The more consecrated a thing or person is, the stronger God's presence and grace for us through it is. Just as there were three increasingly consecrated orders, or ranks, in Judaism that structured God's people and maintained their unity—Levites, priests, and high priests—there are three degrees of increasingly consecrated orders in the Catholic sacrament of holy orders: the episcopacy, presbyterate, and diaconate (see Acts 14:23; 1 Timothy 3; CCC 1536, 1548, 1554), usually referred to as bishops, priests, and deacons. Just as the Old Testament Levites and priests derived their authority from the high priest, who received it from God, our deacons and priests serve under the authority of the bishop and his apostolic succession under Christ.

We know from the earliest writings of Church history that the hierarchical structure of the Catholic Church was built on the apostles' understanding of Jewish hierarchy, specifically to safeguard the unity of the Church against the "shameful and detestable sedition, utterly abhorrent to the elect of God" that they anticipated among the members of Christ's Church.[16]

St. Ignatius of Antioch, who is known as the Doctor of Unity, taught as early as the first century that a bishop should be obeyed as Christ:

> See that you all follow the bishop, even as Jesus Christ does the Father, and the presbytery as you would the apostles; and reverence the deacons, as being the institution of God. Let no man do anything connected with the Church without the bishop ... Wherever the bishop shall appear, there let the multitude [of the people] also be; even as, wherever Jesus Christ is, there is the Catholic Church ... whatsoever [the bishop] shall approve of, that is also pleasing to God, so that everything that is done may be secure and valid.[17]

St. Ignatius goes on to say:

> Let all things therefore be done by you with good order in Christ. Let the laity be subject to the deacons; the deacons to the presbyters; the presbyters to the bishop; the bishop to Christ, even as he is to the Father.[18]

In another letter, he notes that "apart from these, there is no Church ... he who does anything apart from the bishop, and presbytery, and deacons, such a man is not pure in his conscience."[19]

Through the writings of the Church Fathers, we see that as the Church expanded, the hierarchy expanded out of necessity, just as it had in Judaism. Non-Catholics will say such writings from Church history are not authoritative because they are not scriptural. We will address that assertion in a later chapter along with what to do about "bad" priests.

But in the meantime, what these quotes absolutely demonstrate is the early Church's understanding of Church hierarchy. Just as neither Moses nor Aaron was the "only mediator" of God's people in the Old Testament, Jesus' high priesthood is not offended by the hierarchy of the Catholic priesthood, but is carried out through them and their helpers in the diaconate. Just like in the Old Testament, women and other laity have their own roles, which are not fulfilled when they have been abdicated by their occupants in the age-old clamor for superiority.

"THE PEOPLE RULE"

Although latent in all times of Church history, Scripture relays that in the end times, the Church will be characterized by defiance in and against the institutional priesthood in particular and against authority in general. The prevailing attitude of rebellion will cause the whole people of God to grow apathetic and decay from within to the point that Christ will "reprove" and "chasten" them. "And to the angel of the church in Laodicea, write ... Because you are lukewarm, and neither cold nor hot, I will spew you out of my mouth" (Revelation 3:14, 16).

As is true of all apocalyptic and prophetic biblical literature, the seven churches in Revelation existed at the time of St. John's writing, but they have a secondary application as well. Throughout Church history, they have also been understood as symbolic of the seven periods of Church history, culminating with the church in Laodicea, meaning "the people rebel."[20]

We all experience great temptations to predicate obedience on our personal estimation of our superiors, but we must not fool ourselves by believing such self-will is true obedience to God. God provides the means with which to disagree with hierarchy when it is proper to do so—and sometimes it is. But the most egregious offense in biblical history arose from a dissent from the institutional priesthood, resulting in a return to bondage and disappearance altogether within five hundred years.

LET'S REVIEW

This is why the Catholic Church has a priesthood:

- Through the Old Testament Tabernacle, God communicated his desire to be served by both an ordained and a lay priesthood.

- God did not change his mind about ordained priesthood: "For I the LORD do not change" (Malachi 3:6). In him, "there is no variation or shadow due to change" (James 1:17). The Old Testament priesthood was not eliminated, but "changed" to include the saving grace of Jesus (see Hebrews 7:11-19).

- The Old Testament priesthood was fulfilled in Jesus as our High Priest (Hebrews 7:19).

- Ezekiel's prophecy of the messianic Temple includes both the ordained and the lay priesthood; therefore, the Church must also include both (see Ezekiel 44).

- Through his body, the Church, Jesus brings the perpetuity of office required of the ordained priesthood forward into the Church, just as he does the lay priesthood in us.

- We cannot live in the closest possible relationship to God if our worship does not include both the ordained and lay priesthoods.

INVITATION

In the Old Testament, God revealed his desire for perpetual liturgical worship facilitated by an institutional priesthood. While the Old Testament priesthood was interrupted by death and ended with the eternal high priesthood of Jesus, his priesthood is carried forth into the world in New Testament history through the priesthood of the Catholic Church. The duty of a priest is to offer sacrifice. Although the common priesthood of all the baptized differs from the ordained priesthood, all are called to offer sacrifices to God. We do this by giving due diligence to the duties of our vocation in life and by "offering up" our own daily sacrifices in union with Christ's perfect, all-redemptive sacrifice. This is especially appropriate in the Mass, where Jesus makes his eternal sacrifice present to us and we offer ourselves as living sacrifices to God. Let us pray.

God Prompt – LOVE the Word ™

 LISTEN: "Like living stones be yourselves built into a spiritual house, to be a holy priesthood, to offer spiritual sacrifices acceptable to God through Jesus Christ ... But you are a chosen race, a royal priesthood, a holy nation, God's own people, that you may declare the wonderful deeds of him who called you out of darkness into his marvelous light" (1 Peter 2:5-9).

 OBSERVE: What habit(s) do you allow that prevent you from fully serving or sacrificing for God as you desire?

Have you ever been guilty of murmuring against your local priest or against Church leadership?

What has God taught us about this in this chapter?

VERBALIZE: Lord, the most meaningful passage of Scripture through which you spoke to me today was ...

Lord, I believe that in response to my reading in this chapter, you want me to ...

As I think about my relationship to the priesthood and with priests I have known ...

I need your help to ...

 ENTRUST: *O Jesus, I pray for more faithful and fervent priests; for your unfaithful and tepid priests; for your priests laboring at home or abroad in distant mission fields; for your tempted priests; for your lonely and desolate priests; for your young priests; for your dying priests; for the souls of your priests in purgatory. But above all, I recommend to you the priests dearest to me: the priest who baptized me; the priests who absolved me from my sins; the priests at whose Masses I assisted and who gave me your Body and Blood in Holy Communion; the priests who taught and instructed me; all the priests to whom I am indebted in any other way (especially ...). O Jesus, keep them all close to your heart and bless them abundantly in time and in eternity. Amen. – "Daily Prayer for Priests," St. Thérèse of Lisieux*

Sacrificial Love

The Bronze Altar Is Fulfilled in the Cross

*I*srael entered into covenant with God at Sinai, and Moses, as the mediator of the covenant, sealed it by sprinkling both the Book of the Covenant and the people with sacrificial blood. The Tabernacle was made and set up according to the pattern shown to Moses on a thundering, flaming, trembling Mount Sinai. Now God is present with and dwells with mankind in a special way, manifesting his will from the hushed silence of "the tent of meeting." The priesthood has been called and consecrated. The Tabernacle is the place of relationship with God, signifying he is a God of presence and sacrifice who calls his people into presence with him through sacrifices of their own.

At this point, we are ready to turn to the Tabernacle structure itself, and its furniture, trappings, rituals, and practices. The bronze altar, also called the "brazen altar" or "altar of sacrifice," was situated right inside the courtyard upon entering the gate to the Tabernacle. The Hebrew root for altar means "place of slaughter." The "altar" (from the Latin *alta,* meaning "high") is a "high place for sacrifice or slaughter." The Tabernacle altar was raised on a mound of earth, higher than the surrounding implements, foreshadowing how Christ, our sacrifice, would also be lifted up: "so must the Son of man be lifted up, that whoever believes in him may have eternal life" (John 3:14-15). Jesus' altar was a Roman cross on a hill (Golgotha) overlooking the Temple of sacrifice in Jerusalem.

Measuring seven-and-a-half feet square and four-and-a-half feet deep, the Tabernacle altar was made of acacia tree wood overlaid with bronze (symbolic of judgment). Horns projected from each corner, and a bronze grate was inset to hold the animal. The altar was the place for burning animal sacrifices and pouring out their blood, illustrating that atonement for sin was the first thing necessary to approach God. "You shall give life for life" (Exodus 21:23-24).

Try to imagine the number of sacrifices offered daily on the altar and the accompanying odor, blood, and flies. Take a moment to appreciate that as an Israelite, your sin causes something to die right in front of you; in fact, you have to kill it yourself. Would you not grasp in the most literal way that "the wages of sin is death" (Romans 6:23)? Would you not think long and hard before sinning on purpose? Why do you think the people felt a relationship with God was worth the death of all those animals? What did they know about him that we do not?

These sacrifices and their accompanying rituals—the details of which are found in the book of Leviticus—made a relationship with God possible for the people. Although the number and detail of the sacrifices can sometimes provoke feelings of oppression and even disgust, God's concern for his people and his desire for communion with them become increasingly clear to anyone who carefully reads the Bible. Each detailed regulation recorded in the Torah reveals something of God for the people, so that the ceremonial laws provided the framework through which the Israelites understood how to relate to God.

The number of regulations governing all the various sacrifices (what was clean and unclean, the rules and rubrics, and the detailed awareness and prescriptions for which sins required which sacrifices) can make reading through Leviticus quite overwhelming. Consider it as you might the tax code, and you get a general idea of Leviticus' purpose and why it can be so challenging to read. Unless you are a priest with a love and gift for the Liturgy, a similar attempt to read the rubrics for Mass would probably prove just as difficult.

In fact, a non-Catholic might pick up a Roman Missal and conclude such a document has nothing whatsoever to do with a personal, spiritual relationship with God; he might even view the Mass and the Catholic Liturgy as merely a performance with no spiritual value. But when he came to know what the services mean to those who participate in them with faith and awe, he might revise his judgment. Similarly, the value to us in studying Leviticus and the Old Testament sacrificial system centered on the Tabernacle is in the whole picture rather than the details.

The name "Leviticus" is derived from the tribe of Levi, who were a gift and help to the high priesthood. Leviticus gives extensive instructions for the sacrificial system that atoned for both ceremonial and moral impurity so that the people could participate in the purity of the Tabernacle Presence. It was the "worship manual" for the whole people, so that the priesthood would know how to carry out the requirements and responsibilities expected of them. And the knowledge was never exclusive to the priests. When we place all the ceremonial details within the context of God's desire for communion and intimacy with his people, they take on a tender quality in the lengths to which God goes to make peace with his people despite their sins.

The laws for the altar of sacrifice and the offerings held there included both bloody animal sacrifices and food offerings made by fire. The bloody offerings included the burnt offering, peace offering, sin offering, and the guilt, or trespass, offering. The grain, or meal, offering was the only bloodless sacrifice. Perhaps because it most closely prefigures Christ's ultimate sacrifice, or maybe because it was the most common, Leviticus begins with the law of burnt offerings, which were sacrificed daily on the bronze altar. Besides the Day of Atonement for the nation, on which the sin offering was central, the burnt offering was the most important sacrifice on all the major feast days.

Only domestic animals were accepted. Not even a clean (i.e., kosher) animal was permitted if it was wild or taken in hunting, so that the people had to sacrifice what was endeared and valuable to them in its upbringing and labor. This requirement also illustrates that Jesus' sacrifice, as antitype, would not be forced, but free and unresisting.

Equally important is the aspect of degrees of the "cost" of the sacrifices according to the seriousness of the sins. Non-Catholics will often say "sin is sin," and that no particular sin is any worse than another. Aside from the impracticality of such a statement—no one would say speeding is the same as adultery or violent murder— the levitical sacrificial system instituted by God contradicts that assessment. The New Testament also indicates there is "deadly" sin and "not deadly sin," a clear differentiation in seriousness (see 1 John 5:16-17). All such distinctions are outlined in Old Testament sacrificial law.

Some theologians put forth that sacrifice may be older than vocal prayer. Sacrifice *is* prayer, *is* worship, in its simplest and inarticulate form. Satan tempted Jesus with power and fame to worship him, not as a proclamation of verbal allegiance, but in sacrifice (see Matthew 4).

The altar of sacrifice in the Tabernacle faced the Holy of Holies. Because they were wholly consumed, the burnt offerings signified total self-donation to God in praise and love and depicted most clearly the sacrifice of Christ. Therefore, we will look only at the burnt offerings in detail, since we cannot cover them all.

REQUIREMENTS FOR BURNT OFFERINGS

Presentation

There were several steps in the rituals for the various bloody offerings. Repeated, bloody slaughtering of sheep, goats, and pigeons may seem primitive and barbaric to us because we do not understand it. The term "sacrifice" has become almost meaningless to contemporary thought, but an attempt to "feel" the sacrifices the way they are presented to us in Scripture comes as close to an appreciation as we are likely to get.

First, the one offering the sacrifice had to present his own sacrifice and identify himself with it. (As St. Paul later said, "I am crucified with Christ.") He did so publicly to the priest at the Tabernacle. The sacrifice could not simply be a "present" to God; it had to be offered specifically as an atoning sacrifice. The Hebrew word for sacrifice means "offering, or gift," from the root meaning "to bring near." A sacrifice could bring man near to God, but in doing so, it was not merely man's gift to him; it was also God's gift to man, since in the sacrifice, God would draw near to him. The sacrifice brought man and God together, and in the Old Testament, that communion was intimately connected with blood and death. As such, poverty was no impediment to offering sacrifice to God. Provisions were made for those who did not own and were unable to offer an expensive bull or even the less valuable sheep or goat from the flock; instead, they brought birds, as Mary and Joseph offered in the Temple at Jesus' presentation (see Luke 2:22).

The innumerable violent Old Testament sacrifices and scores of dead carcasses were not capable of permanent or eternal atonement for sin, and they were never intended to be (see Galatians 3:23-24). Out of necessity, they had to be repeated until a permanent solution could be offered. But it is vital for us to understand that God does not take pleasure in blood and death. Life and blood belong to God (see Leviticus 17:11).

The emotional, visceral, physical connection to the blood and death of their animals was a megaphone for the absolute, inherent violence of sin; the reality of God's mercy; and most importantly, the foreshadowing of the total self-donation he would make of his own body and blood in his Son, Jesus Christ:

> But in these sacrifices there is a reminder of sin year after year. For it is impossible that the blood of bulls and goats should take away sins. Consequently, when Christ came into the world, he said, "Sacrifices and offerings thou hast not desired, but a body hast thou prepared for me; in burnt offerings and sin offerings thou hast taken no pleasure" (Hebrews 10:3-6).

There were parts of the ceremony in which the priest acted as mediator for the one offering the sacrifice, but the offerer had to make the sacrifice himself. Additionally, it had to take place at the door of the Tent of Meeting, since the Israelites were prone to idolatry at places other than the appointed Tabernacle or Temple—in "fields" and "on high places." The single, central location helped maintain the purity and unity of the people and their worship, especially later when they settled the Promised Land and the Temple was built. Although the sacrifices later required several difficult pilgrimages to the Temple throughout the liturgical year, the central location was invaluable in preserving their religious identity and purity of worship. Then, there were multiple sacrifices at one location; now, there has been a reversal in Christ: only one sacrifice, but offered everywhere (see Malachi 1:11).

This single, perfect sacrifice serves as a similar unifier and preservative for the Catholic Church. Unlike Protestants, Catholics go to church to be with and receive Jesus literally, present in the Holy Eucharist. The homily or sermon, church building, music and programs (or lack thereof) may be "good," or not; local parishes, pastors, and people may be warm and welcoming and supportive of our needs, or not; they may or may not be dysfunctional or have personal agendas. But for Catholics, none of that changes our fundamental reason for going to church. We go there to receive Jesus' perfect sacrifice for the atonement of our sins, because that is where he offers it for us. Going to a specific place matters; we do not just "do our own thing with God" in the woods or on the beach or by staying home and watching a service on television, or whatever else feels more personally enriching. As Catholics, we go to the place where Jesus gives himself to us: church—because in Mass, Jesus is in the Eucharist.

Laying on of Hands

Beyond the location and individual responsibility of the offerer, the second step of the sacrifice was the "laying on of the hand," a ceremony specific to bloody offerings. "He shall lay his hand upon the head of the burnt offering, and it shall be accepted for him to make atonement for him" (Leviticus 1:4). The worshiper had to put his hands "with all his might" between the horns of the beast, identifying himself with his gift and spiritually dying with it, so that the mediating animal put him back into fellowship with God. This deeper meaning may have been more than the one offering consciously realized or even intended, but it was that toward which the action pointed.

The ceremonial hand-laying included a public confession of sin and indicated the transferral of specific sins to the animal being sacrificed in place of the one offering sacrifice (see Levitcus 16:21). In a sense, it was a "pre-sacrament," as a transfer or communication of something invisible through a visible act. On the Day of Atonement, Aaron placed his hands on the head of one of the goats of the sin offering to "confess over him all the iniquities of the people of Israel," so that the nation's iniquity was symbolically transferred from Israel to the goat. While there is no specific mention of confession in the biblical ritual for the burnt offering, Rabbinical tradition holds that it was customary to confess over the victim for the burnt offering. The people confessed their sins to the priest, who offered sacrifices on their behalf, but God considered himself to be the recipient of the confession and the sacrifice as well as the author of their forgiveness. There was no sacrifice, no restitution, no atonement possible at all for intentional sin (see Numbers 15:30-31).

The obvious need for a priest's mediation on behalf of the sins of the entire community is a major reason why I embraced the Catholic Church. As a Protestant leader, I endured the devastating effects of multiple church splits. A few who led such rebellions later said that they had confessed and repented to God, that he had forgiven them and that they were "right before him," and that their responsibility and guilt for ruining two church families and two pastors' family finances and reputations were therefore removed, making discussion about it illegitimate. However, I personally experienced why that could not end the matter because I was part of the church they had destroyed, and they had not asked *me* or the pastor or any of the rest of us for forgiveness or made any attempt at restitution.

When a Christian sins, he sins against God and the whole community (see 1 Corinthians 12:26). Just as God prescribed in the Old Testament and was depicted through the laying of hands on the sacrificial victim, when a Catholic goes to confession, he confesses his guilt to God through the priest, who represents both God and the whole Church, and he is forgiven on behalf of both (see John 20:23). In the early Church, this was done in the public assembly. Not until several hundred years later did the practice of more private confession and absolution become available.

When you imagine this process for yourself, you realize that the laying on of hands ceremony taught and expressed several grave and inescapable realities for the people. The Hebrew verb used does not merely mean to lay the hand on, but to rest or lean heavily upon the victim, "Thy wrath *lies heavily* upon me" (Psalm 88:7, emphasis added).

The offerer must "rely heavily" on the victim to receive absolution from God in exchange for the sacrifice; he must confess his personal sin; he must accept God's judgment against his sin; he must ask for God's mercy in allowing his guilt and sin-debt to transfer to the sacrificial animal; and finally, he must trust in God's promise of atonement for his sin in obeying the divine conditions for it: "It shall be accepted for him to make atonement for him" (Leviticus 1:4). So, too, we plead the blood of "the Lamb of God, who takes away the sin of the world" (John 1:29).

Slaughter

The third step was the actual slaughter of the animal, and the ritual was the same for all the bloody offerings. Again, in sacrifices for personal sin, the sacrificial animal was killed by the sinner himself "before the LORD," at the door of the Tabernacle. In death, the life, through the blood, was released from the body, poured out at the base of the altar and given over to God who gave it first. To a Hebrew, the soul was not "the spiritual part of a person," as we associate the soul to be. To him, man does not have a soul, he *is* a soul. His soul is visible in body and "invisible" as life in his blood. If one is also guilty of the whole Law if he breaks even one part (see James 2:10), then not only must his lifeblood be poured out, but his body must be given over to death, too.

Today, it is rare to kill an animal that belongs to us. Agricultural communities have always been intimately bound to their flocks and herds, as their survival depended on them. These sacrifices would have been taken from animals known by name—pets of sorts—both valuable and dear. But why blood, and why such a valuable animal? There is something mysterious and dreadfully potent about blood that is separated from the body, never to return. The awfulness of our estrangement from God becomes particularly striking and clear in the slaughter, especially as the offerer is identified with it in the laying on of the hand.

The priest presented the blood of the sacrifice to God by sprinkling it "round about against the altar that is at the door of the tent of meeting" (Leviticus 1:5); this completed the atonement. All of the blood poured out on the altar represented life, "for the life of the flesh is in the blood," God said, "and I have given it for you upon the altar to make atonement for your souls; for it is the blood that makes atonement, by reason of the life" (Leviticus 17:11). Life in exchange for life, the life of an innocent victim in atonement for the life of the sinner: "Without the shedding of blood there is no forgiveness of sins" (Hebrews 9:22). The daily bloody sacrifices occurring at the altar were a constant, shocking reminder for the people of the exorbitant cost of sin.

Because the Cross can sometimes feel removed from us by history, culture, and familiarity, we do not always appreciate that for us, too, "the wages of sin is death" (Romans 6:23) until our individual death approaches, if we appreciate it at all. Because God is pure and eternal, a single sin against him requires a pure and eternal sacrifice as atonement. As finite creatures, we cannot offer an *eternal* sacrifice, either of ourselves or of an animal or of anything created at all; as sinful creatures, we cannot offer a perfectly *pure* sacrifice. "For it is impossible that the blood of bulls and goats should take away sins" (Hebrews 10:4). Animal sacrifices were only ever meant to be a temporary mercy until the one, pure, and eternal sacrifice in Christ could be made. As eternal high priest and spotless victim, "by a single offering he has perfected for all time those who are sanctified" (Hebrews 10:14).

Burning

At this point in the offering, the priest burned the sacrifice. The smoke from these offerings ascended heavenward in the fire of the altar at the door of the Tabernacle as a "pleasing odor to the LORD" (Leviticus 1:9). This complete incineration in fire foreshadowed the total sacrifice of Christ on the Cross and, by extension, that the worshiper must hold nothing back when coming to God; everything is consumed in the relationship between God and the worshiper.

John the Baptist summed up the entire Old Testament sacrificial system and struck the concert pitch of the New Testament when he cried for repentance: "Behold the Lamb of God, who takes away the sin of the world!" (John 1:29). As blood signified the Old Testament, so it does in the New Testament. Jesus said, "This is my blood of the covenant, which is poured out for many for the forgiveness of sins" (Matthew 26:28). Jesus uses specific sacrificial terminology from the Old Testament in "pouring out" of the sacrificial blood on the altar. Paul also connects Jesus' sacrifice to those of the Old Testament when he says Christ "gave himself up for us, a fragrant offering and sacrifice to God" (Ephesians 5:2), and that "we have redemption through his blood, the forgiveness of our trespasses, according to the riches of his grace" (Ephesians 1:7).

St. Peter also uses levitical language when he teaches that we were redeemed with precious blood, as of a lamb without blemish and without spot, the blood of Christ. He adds that Christ, although manifested at the end of the times, was foreknown as the Lamb of God before the foundation of the world (see 1 Peter 1:18-20). St. John, too, speaks in the language of Leviticus when he declares that "the blood of Jesus ... cleanses us from all sin" (1 John 1:7). Even in Revelation, where we see Jesus glorified, he appears as a Lamb that had been slain, both alive and dead, simultaneously.

Sacrificial Meal

As if to indicate how difficult sacrifice can be, daily private offerings were usually accompanied by refreshment. The covenant was ratified in a sacrificial offering, after which the people "ate and drank" before God in covenant fellowship (see Exodus 24:11), so the communal meal was an integral part of the sacrificial system. These Old Testament "cereal offerings" with oil (bread!) and wine were the basis of the *"agape* meal" or "the breaking of bread" (Acts 2:42-46), the Mass of the early Church.[21] Worshipers brought their offerings to the holy table, the presiding minister took whatever was necessary for the meal, and the rest was given to the poor and needy. In the same way that no one ate and drank in the Old Testament except those of the covenant, only Catholics partake of the Eucharist, which *is* the covenant in Jesus' Body and Blood.[22]

Remember that burnt sacrifices occurred morning and night. Although Leviticus is mostly concerned with the basic outlines of the sacrifices and not necessarily the thoughts, emotions, or other practices surrounding them, we know they would all have been accompanied by prayers, praises, penitence, and dances. In fact, the Kohathites, one of the three divisions of the tribe of Levi, were responsible for the music of the Tabernacle (see 1 Chronicles 6:31-48), which helped illustrate what sacrifice meant to an Israelite of the Old Testament. They were bloody and brutal, but they were festive in thanksgiving for God's mercy.

The meal offerings, as all offerings made by fire, never included leaven (see Levitcus 2:11), a biblical symbol of the self-propagation of sin and spiritual corruption. St. Paul charged the Corinthians to purge themselves of the old leaven and then "keep the feast," not with the leaven of malice and wickedness, but with the unleavened bread of sincerity and truth (see 1 Corinthians 5:7).

Produced from crops cultivated from the soil that represented the fruit of man's labor, the grain offering was not offered to God until after it had been ground, sifted, and often cooked—i.e., fully prepared as food. As the burnt offering represented the consecration of the life and the person to God, the meal offering represented the consecration of the fruit of his labors. The one sacrifice provided everything necessary for his offering: the animal, grain, salt, wine, oil, and incense. This shows we must surrender our entire being to the Lord without reserve, along with all our works.

Each of us contributes his or her own time, talent, and treasure in working for God's kingdom. The meal offering reminds us that the fruit of all our labor comes from and ascends back to God. Everything about the Israelite's life was an offering to him in the context of the

Tabernacle. God's claim for full consecration of all our activities covers everything, even to the very food we eat. How does this relate to us in our faith today? Some of us are willing to give "church time" to God, but do not necessarily acknowledge that our "secular life" is due to him as well. But it is all one life. "Whether you eat or drink, or whatever you do, do all to the glory of God" (1 Corinthians 10:31).

While there were some foods that only the rich could afford to eat, grain and olive oil were staples used by every Israelite. The grain offering could only be wheat, just like the hosts for the Eucharist, because wheat in Israel (and now) was the most valued of all the grains. People must not only offer God the fruit of their labor, but the best *result* of their labors—from the gross, not net—and certainly not that which is left over after the bills are paid. We see the Jewish understanding of the principle of giving God one's best when King David proclaimed, "I will not offer burnt offerings to the LORD my God which cost me nothing" (2 Samuel 24:24). No one is exempt from owing God the work of his hands, the food he eats; everything is to be offered to him in sacrifice. In levitical symbolism, consecration of a part signified consecration of the whole. And St. Paul later writes, "For if the dough offered as first fruits is holy, so is the whole lump" (Romans 11:16).

Worth Your Salt

The last requirement for the meal offering was salt (see Leviticus 2:13). As leaven is a principle of impermanence and decay, so salt cures and prevents corruption. This ingredient, necessary for life, was so expensive in ancient times that Roman soldiers were sometimes paid with it, leading to the saying, "he is worth his salt." Indispensable for seasoning food, salt is also a preservative, and was used medicinally as an antiseptic. Newborn babies were rubbed with salt (see Ezekiel 16:4). Water was cleansed and purified with salt (see 2 Kings 2:19-20). Salt was also symbolic of fellowship.

The same Arabic word is used for "salt" and "treaty," so that the expression "a covenant in salt" was used to designate a permanent and inviolable bond, as illustrated in the traditional Arabic expression, "There is salt between us." By nomadic custom, those who have partaken of the same meal or "taken salt together" are regarded as united by an unbreakable bond of friendship or treaty, even upon death.

Numbers 18:19 speaks of the Old Testament offerings as "a covenant of salt for ever before the LORD." This phrase is used similarly to describe God's covenant of eternal kingship with David through his descendants (see 2 Chronicles 13:5). Because salt is symbolic of purification, endurance, preservation, and freedom from corruption, entering into a "covenant of salt" meant binding oneself to another in utmost loyalty and fidelity until death. Such a covenant was never entered into lightly or haphazardly.

The use of salt and salt covenants in the Bible indicates the everlasting nature of the relationship between the "children of salt" and their God. As a preservative, salt prevents decay and corruption and was an indispensable ingredient in all Old Testament sacrificial offerings, symbolizing at every juncture the incorruptibility of God's covenant with his people. According to St. Jerome, Jesus called his disciples "the salt of the earth" (Matthew 5:13) in the Sermon on the Mount "because by the Apostles the whole human race is seasoned."[23]

Like the bloody offerings, the meal offering was brought to God by the offerer himself. The consecration of our works, like the consecration of our persons, must be our own voluntary act. Yet the offering must be delivered through the mediation of the priest; the offerer must not presume himself to lay it on the altar. The remaining and larger portion of the meal offering was given to the priest. As the servant of God in the work of his house, he was set apart from secular occupations to be wholly given to the duties of this office.

The Hebrew word for "consecration" is derived from the verb "to fill," which gave rise to the expression "to fill the hand." In turn, this came to be a liturgical expression meaning "to confer power," "to institute to a priestly office," and therefore, "to consecrate." The basic idea conveyed by the rites and words is the conferment of a certain power.

In a physical sense, the priests' hands would be filled solely with sacrifices as they served God in the Tabernacle, but more importantly, their consecration meant that their hands would always be filled with service to God to the exclusion of everything else. God alone would be their portion. In order to support them, God commanded that parts of various offerings should be given to the priests. This is the basis for why Catholic priests receive a "stipend" for each Mass they celebrate.

The whole burnt offering, where the entire gift was given over to God was an act of sacrifice, worship, and thanksgiving, of *eucharist.* The sin offerings were an act of penitence; the peace offerings, accompanied by a communal meal, were an act of communion. In sacrifice, thanksgiving, and communion, we see the three supreme moments of the Mass. The Catholic Church is the only church in which these remain literal—now, three in One. *Eucharista.*

A PROPER DISPOSITION

"Pure offering" denotes pure spiritual sacrifice, unmarred by mixed motives. The blood of bulls and goats could never have taken away sin, even temporarily, apart from the penitence and faith of the worshiping people. The Old Testament was not a superstitious or primitive system, despite our modern views (see Sirach 34:14-19). If one sacrifices from what has been wrongfully obtained or gives with ulterior motives, the offering is impure. The gifts of the lawless are not acceptable (see Genesis 4:3-16). Even where the requirements are fully met (if that were even possible), God is not obligated by them! I cannot "earn" atonement from him, even were I able to keep the Law, as the Rich Young Man learned from Jesus (see Matthew 19:16-26); no number or multitude of sacrifices *obligates* God to spare me in mercy, even now.

The Old Testament Law required that sacrifice be the outward expression of an inward disposition. The prophets denounced as spiritually empty sacrifices that were not an expression of the heart of the worshiper (see Psalm 50). The Hebrew *believed* that if he came before God in the appointed ways and in the right spirit, he would be accepted by God and have communion with him and the whole people. The psalms indicate that he not only believed this, but experienced it, "As far as the east is from the west, so far does he remove our transgressions from us" (Psalm 103:12).

As I was praying through the sorrowful mysteries of the Rosary recently, it occurred to me that I have always seen Jesus' atoning sacrifice for me in terms of a negative benefit: Jesus' sacrifice *took away* the eternal punishment for sin. But I realized that morning that Jesus' sacrifice did not just save me from God's wrath and punishment. The wholly consumed, pure sacrifice of Jesus also made possible every benefit and blessing I have ever experienced: the joy of saying my wedding vows on trembling legs, the searing love of holding my newborns, the streaking bliss of my husband's kiss, pounding waves on the shore, tremors of glory in Vivaldi's violin, and the Christmas morning giddiness of holding my first published book. Jesus was a burnt offering because his sacrifice was entire from first breath to last, every moment lived perfectly in the Law and God's will, and every single one of those purest of breaths offered back to the Father.

The sacred offerings in the Old Testament were the very presence of the offerer before God on the altar, not merely a reminder of some distant and shadowy performance of the past. Through these sacrifices, a memorial unto God (what was remembered) was brought up from the past to the present. This is why the Eucharist is both the true memorial and true sacrifice of Christ. Jesus' command to "do this in remembrance of me" brings his sacrifice into the present. We experience his abiding presence on earth in the Eucharist. The "pure offering" in the historical passion of Christ for the life of the world is brought to our hearts and to our lips.

DAY OF ATONEMENT

The Day of Atonement is considered by the Jews to be the date on which Moses received the second set of Ten Commandments, at which time the Israelites were granted atonement for the sin of the golden calf; hence, its designation as *the* Day of Atonement.[24]

Like all the levitical stipulations, the provisions for this highest holy day of the year in Judaism might appear very primitive and unspiritual to a modern reader if separated from their fulfillment in Christ. Known as "the fast" (Acts 27:9), the Day of Atonement was kept as a Sabbath and a fast day, and was the only one prescribed for the whole congregation. All sins were confessed in the plural (we have done this, we have done that), emphasizing communal responsibility and communal atonement for sins.

The national atonement feast, *Yom Kippur* in Hebrew, only atoned for sins between man and God, not for sins between individual people. An individual was responsible for atoning for sins against another person and pursuing reconciliation with that person before the Day of Atonement, righting the wrongs committed against him if possible, as Jesus taught in the Sermon on the Mount (see Matthew 5:24).

Far from the modern idea that God is so kind and merciful that he may be approached at any time, in any posture, and in the most familiar terms, the Hebrews understood the presence of God to be so dangerous that it would kill a man if he drew near with presumption or lack of preparation. "It is a fearful thing to fall into the hands of the living God" (Hebrews 10:31). Only at one hour, one day a year—and only then after significant ritual and moral purification and precaution in body and mind—did the high priest dare to pass behind the veil into the Presence manifesting there.

The bells on the hem of the high priest's liturgical robe indicated all was well as he carried out his solemn duties for the people, but it has been said that there was a rope tied around his ankle in the event he died so he could be removed from the Holy of Holies without anyone else entering. As incense drifted up and over the veil, he entered the dark mystery of the Holy of Holies alone. With his finger, he sprinkled the blood of the sacrifice of atonement for the people on the mercy seat *where the cloud was* without touching it (see Hebrews 9:6). I wonder what he saw, what he heard, what he felt.

Because the mercy seat received the sacrificial blood of atonement for the whole people, it was also called the seat of "propitiation," meaning "satisfaction," as in satisfaction for sin. It was a massive plate of gold that served as a cover for the Ark and formed one piece with the cherubim that rose from it above the Ark. The divine glory, the *Shekinah,* dwelt there between the cherubim.

The Day of Atonement was the only day the sacred name of God, revealed to Moses, could be spoken aloud. Called the excellent name, the great name, the only name, the glorious and terrible name, the hidden and mysterious name, the name of the substance, the proper name, and most frequently, the explicit or the separated name,[25] the high priest proclaimed the Great Name over the people, and it was done so in the form of a blessing. God blesses you also with his name: "In the name of the Father, and of the Son, and of the Holy Spirit."

We know from reading the levitical text what was to be done and how, what was prayed, what ideas and emotions surrounded the rite, and what it meant to those who participated in it. Any euphoria of spiritual worship is left to our imagination, except in Sirach, where the high priest is described in soaring praise: "How glorious he was when the people gathered round him as he came out of the inner sanctuary!" (Sirach 50:5). Through him the full wonder and mystery of Temple worship on the Day of Atonement occurred, when he came forth from the "house of the veil," the Holy of Holies, to offer the burnt sacrifice.

And perhaps nowhere more beautifully than through the sacrifice of the Day of Atonement, Leviticus gives us the language with which to speak of Christ, who is, in his person and blood, our "propitiation" and mercy seat (see Romans 3:25). The mercy seat and altar are united in Christ's "at-one-ment." As St. Ignatius says, Jesus is our altar in his very person.[26] In receiving him, we receive the kiss of God's mercy and judgment (see Psalm 85:10). To "be reconciled to God" (2 Corinthians 5:20) means to be "at one" with him. The dry, difficult regulations of Leviticus have overflowed their potential in the poetic promise of Christ, in whom the Old Testament *came true*.

LET'S REVIEW

This is why the Catholic Church has a real altar:

- The Old Testament Tabernacle altar communicated God's desire for sacrificial worship that mirrors and communicates his own sacrificial love.

- The required atonement for sin is "life for life," to illustrate the reality that sin always causes death (see Romans 6:23).

- Old Testament sacrifices of blood and goats could not make eternal atonement for sin against an eternal God because the sacrifices themselves were not eternal (see Hebrews 10:4).

- Jesus' one eternal sacrifice forever brings perfection to those who follow him through grace (see Hebrews 10:14).

- The Catholic priesthood offers a real group sacrifice for group worship, which requires a consecrated altar.

- At Jesus' command, the Catholic priesthood has always offered the only true sacrifice possible on Catholic altars, that of the Body and Blood of Christ himself (see Luke 22:19-20).

- Jesus promises his sacrifice is applied to our lives every time we receive the Eucharist (see John 6:56-58).

- We participate in Jesus' sacrifice by offering up our own sacrifices in union with his, and they become redemptive through his grace.

INVITATION

Through the altar of sacrifice in the Tabernacle, God was teaching his people that their sins would always end in blood and death. Every sin against the eternal God, no matter how small, requires an eternal sacrifice for atonement, which finite creatures can never make. Rather than requiring the death of every guilty person, in which case we would all be lost, God, in his mercy, allowed the guilt and punishment to be transferred to an animal of great value to the penitent. Proper worship demanded that the people accept their guilt through confession of sin to the priest and through the spilling of blood. Only through this ritual were the people able to make satisfaction to God for sin. But this was a temporary solution. Additionally, although atonement for unintentional or venial sin was possible and provided for, there was no Old Testament provision for presumptuous sin. Aren't you thankful to live in the Church age of grace and mercy? Doesn't that make you want to strive for holiness in thanksgiving to God? Let us pray.

God Prompt – LOVE the Word ™

 LISTEN: "Has the LORD as great delight in burnt offerings and sacrifices, as in obeying the voice of the LORD? Behold, to obey is better than sacrifice, and to hearken than the fat of rams. For rebellion is as the sin of divination, and stubbornness is as iniquity and idolatry" (1 Samuel 15:22-23).

 OBSERVE: What was the most recent thing you clearly remember God asking you to do?

Did you do it? Why, or why not?

Have you given your life completely and wholeheartedly to him in exchange for his sacrifice on the Cross? Reflect.

Where might you be holding back or resisting a complete sacrifice of your life, circumstances, or possessions? Right now, ask God to reveal any areas to which he wants total access that you have not granted him.

Are you guilty of attending Mass or offering other sacrifices without heartfelt deliberation and attention or without the necessary love of neighbor that God requires? Reflect.

 VERBALIZE: Lord, the most meaningful passage of Scripture through which you spoke to me today was ...

Lord, I believe that in response to my reading in this chapter, you want me to ...

As I think about my obedience to you, which is better than my sacrifices for you, I worry about ...

 ENTRUST: *Lord, how thankful I am that you gave your life as payment for my sins. Make me truly sorry for the effects of my sins, that I might never sin again. Help me remember at every Mass what it means that your Body was broken and your Blood was poured out for me on the altar of the Cross. Teach me to consider my sacrificial suffering, in union with yours, to be spiritually powerful. Amen.*

Perfected by His Presence

The Altar Fire Is Fulfilled in Purgatory

*N*umerous sacred events in Old Testament history constructed the Hebrew association between fire and God's presence over time. God continually revealed himself, parented, spoke, rescued, led, and instructed his people through fire in a divine "progressive pedagogy."

Moses received his call from God in the burning bush. The Passover lambs were roasted in fire. The pillar of fire guided God's people through the wilderness to Sinai. With great reverence for God's presence in the fire, Moses received the covenant there, instructions that included the Tabernacle and altar preparations. The first offerings made upon the bronze altar on behalf of the people were accompanied by fire fall. Throughout the Old Testament, God accepted offerings and carried out judgments through fire.

The burnt offering was the only sacrifice completely consumed when placed on the altar. The word "holocaust" in Hebrew literally means "burnt offering, going up to God, ascending, wholly burned." The burnt offerings had to be male, unblemished, and freely offered, then brought to God at the door of the Tabernacle (see Leviticus 1:3).

The animal's blood was poured out at the base of the altar, while the meat was entirely burned up so that God could receive the sacrifice as a pleasant aroma (see Leviticus 1:9). Only the best animals without defect were acceptable (see Leviticus 22:18-33).

Seen in the light of the fulfillment for which they were intended—Jesus as the High Priest of the New Covenant (see Hebrews 4:14)—the levitical stipulations for brutal, bloody sacrifice take on a new meaning. They are not meant to illustrate that God was violent or bloodthirsty. Rather, they bear the tenderness of a God who longs to have us near him. As the fulfillment of burnt sacrifices of the Old Testament, Jesus' life was totally consumed, even unto death (see Hebrews 4:15). As the Only Begotten Son of the Father (see John 3:16), Jesus is the first and best of God's livelihood and a willing sacrifice (John 10:17-18).

We study the Old Testament in order to more completely understand the type of worship that is pleasing to God, how Jesus fulfilled those requirements for us, and, therefore, how to please God in our worship in his Church. As the only offerings that were wholly consumed on the altar when accepted, the sacrificial burnt offerings of the Old Testament indicate to us that nothing is to be held back when we worship God. Sacrificial worship draws us closest to God. In obeying Jesus' command to receive his sacrifice (see John 6), our own sacrifices must also be freely made of the best we have and are.

The sacrifices in the Old Testament prepare us to recognize with familiarity the ultimate sacrifice of Jesus, our High Priest. Offered on the Cross, his sacrifice continues presently on the altars of every Catholic Church every day, at every hour, throughout the world until he returns. We are commanded to imitate Christ by offering the sacrifice of our very selves, united with his at every Mass in which we participate. When we offer ourselves to God, he takes us at his word, and in a sense, he falls on us in "altar fire."

A SWEET SAVOR

St. Peter offers the "altar fire" explanation to early Christians, who were bewildered by the suffering inherent in being Christian. Possibly their suffering seemed to them particularly intense, unfair, or aggravated. But St. Peter offers them comfort: "Beloved, do not be surprised at the fiery ordeal which comes upon you to prove you, as though something strange were happening to you" (1 Peter 4:12). St. Peter says fiery trials "test" or "prove" us, not to God, since he already knows what we are made of, and not as a kind of "pass" or "fail" litmus test. Fiery trials reveal to us our faults and weaknesses, so we know where to work with him to grow in holiness:

> The Holy Spirit makes us discern between trials, which are necessary for the growth of the inner man,[27] and temptation, which leads to sin and death.[28] We must also discern between being tempted and consenting to temptation ... God does not want to impose the good, but wants free beings ... There is a certain usefulness to temptation. No one but God knows what our soul has received from him, not even we ourselves. But temptation reveals it in order to teach us to know ourselves, and in this way we discover our evil inclinations and are obliged to give thanks for the goods that temptation has revealed to us[29] (CCC 2847).

Part of the gift of the grace won for us on the Cross is that suffering can now be redemptive in, with, and through Christ, and not simply a punishing and painful experience. God allows both trials and temptations for our good, to strengthen virtue and reveal vice. But the Bible teaches that God does not tempt us to sin. "Let no one say when he is tempted, 'I am tempted by God'; for God cannot be tempted with evil and he himself tempts no one" (James 1:13).

Interestingly, the Greek word translated as "fiery ordeal" in 1 Peter 4:12 is also used in 1 Peter 1:6-7 to speak of the intense fire that purifies metals. St. Peter says suffering can purify us of sin:

> Since therefore Christ suffered in the flesh, arm yourselves with the same thought, for whoever has suffered in the flesh has ceased from sin, so as to live for the rest of the time in the flesh no longer by human passions but by the will of God (1 Peter 4:1-2).

When seen and embraced in this way, suffering ceases to be simply pain; it takes on a redemptive quality as it burns away the impurities of sin and attachments to the things of this world.

AN UNDERMINED FOUNDATION

God has spent my adult life healing the "father wound" I carry. The fear and woundedness I experienced early in my life provoked rage and rebellion in my teens and early twenties, until I realized I would eventually go to jail, forfeit my marriage, and pass this wound to my own children if I did not get myself under control. The problem was, my wound seemed so alive, deeply rooted, and tangled beneath the surface, that I wholly identified the "trunk" of my personality with my anger and hurt and could not see why or how I was responsible. Once I accepted responsibility under God's truth-telling Word (see John 8:32), I worked diligently on my behavior and got my aggression mostly under control. Then, just like the Israelites in the wilderness, God began moving from my outward behavior to my inward motivations and perceptions: What was causing my emotional eruptions? What was motivating my self-medication, irrational reactions, and bondage to toxic relationships?

That I could be free from an overwhelming pain I had carried my whole life became my "promised land," and I was willing to follow Jesus anywhere and do anything he asked in pursuit of it. With his help and under his guidance, I became expert at identifying my "trigger people"; sidestepping those land mines began to happen more swiftly and easily. But then ... well, then things really got interesting.

Rather than experiencing negative relationships that provoked emotional reactions in me, God began sending me holy people who lifted me up. I had no idea how to act. These people triggered me too, only weirdly, since the relationships and circumstances were so positive! My reactions had all the signs of "my daddy thing," as I called it, but why? It was inexplicable. I had absolutely no idea how to go that deep, how to see that far into the abyss of my own soul, much less how to heal it so it would not cause any more problems. God began burrowing deeper, digging way down, drilling even below the bedrock of my issue to the wound beneath. It has been an excruciating purification accompanied by wailing and gnashing of teeth, but he granted me the graces to see how every awful, bewildering, soul-searing step was necessary for a small and specific healing. Today I am free, but that was a fifteen- to twenty-year process, and I still deal with the fallout. Why? Because my father undermined my "attachment bond" with him very early on in my life in ways that caused me to deal with other relationships improperly.

Do you see how sin, whether committed by us or perpetrated against us, can create attachments that must be purified before we are truly free to love and serve God to our full potential? At first I could not serve God because my behavior made me a hypocrite. Once I got that mostly under control, I could not do the sacrificial things he asked of me because I was in too much pain. And I could not give myself wholly to him; I was afraid to take the risk; I did not trust him.

Sin, then, is so much more than simply doing something wrong. The actual definition includes "miss," "blame," "guilt," "mistake," "fault," "loss." God allowed my suffering to trigger behavior that escalated to the degree I finally began asking questions: *What is wrong with me? Why am I doing this?*

Once I started finding answers to these questions, I suffered deeply under the reasons, because I had never been able to really see or acknowledge the soul-piercing truth. My father was incapable of loving me properly. *What is wrong with me that my own parent can't love me?* What an awful realization for anyone to have.

But once God drew me to the awful truth of it and I accepted it, I was invited to erect some boundaries that allowed me to accept my father, faults and all. This is my duty, and my father's right as a child of God, too. All of it involved its own suffering, but with God's grace, I forgave him. Miraculously, I discovered my bitterness and fear, as well as my most common sinful behaviors, were gone. God used my suffering to purify me of a morbidly deep attachment to sin.

Where else is my pain causing me to sin? What is my rage causing me to forfeit? Sin is so much more than just breaking a commandment, or the addictions and habits to which we turn a blind eye. Sin also involves perceptions and motivations, and sometimes those are buried so deeply and so far back in life, that we are unable to manage wholeness ourselves. God sets straight in us what we cannot set right ourselves.

FIRE WITHIN

This process of purification is usually called "sanctification" in Scripture. The word originates from a group of similar Hebrew and Greek words, all from the same root for being "separated" from the world and "consecrated" to God as a sacrificial victim in preparation for a feast day. Because it can be so brutally painful, we struggle against the process of becoming holy and may even feel it is unfair of God, at times, to put us through such torment. But it is like the pain of a surgical procedure—absolutely necessary for life with him—and it is our heavenly Father's great grace, as the letter to the Hebrews teaches us:

In your struggle against sin you have not yet resisted to the point of shedding your blood. And have you forgotten the exhortation which addresses you as sons?—"My son, do not regard lightly the discipline of the Lord, nor lose courage when you are punished by him. For the Lord disciplines him whom he loves, and chastises every son whom he receives." It is for discipline that you have to endure. God is treating you as sons; for what son is there whom his father does not discipline? If you are left without discipline, in which all have participated, then you are illegitimate children and not sons (Hebrews 12:4-8).

In the Old Testament, God punished other nations after their sins had swelled to full measure and spilled over, but he always sent the prophets and disciplined his own people before their sins came to a head. The sufferings God allows in our lives as his children are not meant to destroy us but to train us and fill in our mental, spiritual, and emotional gaps so we are increasingly able to receive him more fully. Scripture is full of depictions of the purification process.

Malachi 3:2 prophesies that God will suddenly enter into his Temple like a blacksmith's fire and a launder's lye, stripping away all the deeply penetrated impurities and dross from the sons of Levi so that their offerings to God will be what they should be. This is a clear indication of some sort of purification directly related to worship and prayer under the Messiah.

Jesus tells us God prunes the fruit-bearing branches of the mystical vine so that they bear even more fruit (see John 15:2). St. Paul speaks of the presence of God transforming us from one glory to another as he draws forth the very image of God himself:

The Day will disclose it, because it will be revealed with fire, and the fire will test what sort of work each one has done. If the work which any man has built on the foundation survives, he will receive a reward. If any man's work is burned up, he will suffer loss, though he himself will be saved, but only as through fire (1 Corinthians 3:13-15).

Paul goes on to say that we are the Temple of which Malachi spoke. The Church calls this process *purgatory*, from a Latin root meaning "to purify." The word "purgatory" is not used in the Bible, but the principle of purification before heaven is found throughout the Bible and Church history. In the biblical texts we have been studying, we have seen this perfecting and purifying process, performed by God himself, described as "fire." This fire purifies us so that we can more fully conform our will to God's will and love more completely. This fire simultaneously destroys and purifies, but in so doing, it accomplishes salvation. "If any man's work is burned up, he will suffer loss, though *he himself will be saved, but only as through fire*" (1 Corinthians 3:15, emphasis added).

The doctrine of purgatory has been part of the Church's teaching for two thousand years. The Fathers of the Church agree that the fire spoken of in 1 Corinthians 3:15 is that of purgatory, which will purify us after death—if we die in the state of grace. When trials are viewed this way, they become our sacred offerings of love, offered in communion with the Cross. Fiery trials, then, are purgatory being accomplished where it should be accomplished: on earth. Even Jesus learned obedience through his suffering (see Hebrews 5:8). This purgatory is the love of God purifying us, and it is the temporal punishment for sin that we are able and required to offer. If we have not cooperated fully with this process during our lives and it is not complete when we die, God finishes it after death, if we remain in his grace upon death. St. Gregory the Great wrote:

> He who is truth says that whoever utters blasphemy against the Holy Spirit will be pardoned neither in this age nor in the age to come. From this sentence we understand that certain offenses can be forgiven in this age, but certain others in the age to come.[30]

St. Catherine of Genoa, called the Apostle of Purgatory, wrote in her Treatise on Purgatory:

> Either in this life or in the life to come, the soul that seeks union with God must be purged by "The fiery Love of God." The holy souls are purged of all the rust and stains of sin which they have not rid themselves in this life. The fire of purgatory is first of all The Fiery Love of God.[31]

St. Faustina agrees, recording in her diary, "I asked these souls what their greatest suffering was. They answered me in one voice that their greatest torment was longing for God."[32]

St. Francis de Sales said:

> The thought of Purgatory is productive rather of consolation than of terror ... Great as the torments of purgatory are ... the interior consolations granted there are nevertheless so ineffable that no earthly bliss and enjoyment can equal them.[33]

Pope Gregory said that the fire of purgatory and the fire of hell are the same fire:

> "Even as in the same fire gold glistens and straw smokes, so in the same fire the sinner burns and the elect is cleansed." Therefore the fire of Purgatory is the same as the fire of hell: and hence they are in the same place.[34]

Gregory of Nyssa said:

> "If one who loves and believes in Christ," has failed to wash away his sins in this life, "he is set free after death by the fire of Purgatory." Therefore there remains some kind of cleansing after this life.[35]

JESUS PAID IT ALL

Non-Catholics often deny the doctrine of purgatory by arguing that the thief on the cross adjacent to Jesus went to paradise immediately and by quoting 2 Corinthians 5:8 as saying, "We would rather be away from the body and at home with the Lord." Neither of these passages disproves the existence of purgatory. Martyrdom is considered a type of "purgatory-in-full," and in the Corinthians passage, Paul says he *would rather be* absent from the body and present with the Lord. But either way, to be in purgatory is to be in God. (More on this shortly.)

A proper understanding of purgatory requires an understanding of Jesus' atonement. "Jesus paid it all" is a line from a hymn I sang and loved as a child. Non-Catholics quote it to me all the time when refuting purgatory. It is certainly true that Jesus paid the eternal debt of sin, a debt that we are unable to satisfy. Even a single sin against an eternal God requires an eternal sacrifice to atone for it. Because we are finite creatures, any sacrifice we make is necessarily limited and therefore inadequate. As the perfect eternal sacrifice, Jesus was both able and willing to make this atoning sacrifice for us. But Jesus left the debt we could pay to us: the earthly debt. If Jesus paid it *all*, then why do we still suffer and ultimately die? The earthly consequence for sin is not "revenge" from God on our sin; it is built into the fabric of the cosmos (see Romans 1:18-31) as surely as gravity.

Stepping out from under the "faucet" of God's saving grace through purposeful, serious sin disconnects us from our end in him. The grace continues to flow from above, but we are no longer standing under it, unless repentance ("to turn away from") and confession return us to that position. Earthly suffering is mere punishment for the nonbeliever, but through Christ, God uses it to discipline and correct (sanctify or purify) his people.

NOT A PLACE

Whatever we call it—salvation, sanctification, purgatory—we see it is a lifelong process of becoming holy that ends in God's arms. Purgatory is not a milder hell, a less joyful heaven, a third place, or a sort of waiting room in between. In fact, purgatory is not a place nor an amount of time at all. Places are of time and matter, both creations of God. God transcends both time and matter as pure Spirit. "To God, all moments of time are present in their immediacy" (CCC 600). As such, he is in all places and times all the time—omnipresent. God exists in a single present moment as "I AM." So rather than a place or amount of time, purgatory is a state of the soul in God. As the *Catechism* elaborates:

> Each man receives his eternal retribution in his immortal soul at the very moment of his death, in a particular judgment that refers his life to Christ: either entrance into the blessedness of heaven—through a purification[36] or immediately[37]—or immediate and everlasting damnation.[38] At the evening of life, we shall be judged on our love"[39] (CCC 1022).

Pope Benedict XVI says that the writings of the mystics did not begin with death and the torments of an exterior purgatory and then show the way to purification and conversion. Rather than a "place" in the depths of the earth with an exterior fire, they saw purgatory as an interior spiritual fire, the soul's experience and awareness of God's immense love and absolute justice. The soul suffers for not having responded appropriately or fully to the perfect love it "sees" and experiences. The soul understands as it was unable to before that the perfect Love extended to it throughout its life *deserves* the soul's lifelong, undivided, all-consuming devotion; anything less is painfully unjust (see 1 Corinthians 3:15). The suffering the soul experiences in "seeing" this love *is* just and is the simple, natural consequence of habitual separation—even teeny tiny separations—of one's will from God's will, which is love. "It is precisely the love of God himself which purifies the soul from the ravages of sin."[40]

HOLOCAUST IS PASSION

In the Bible, fire is used as a symbol for the punitive wrath of God *and* of God's purifying energy and might. When two of Aaron's sons offered "profane fire" with the incense in the Tabernacle, "fire came forth from the presence of the LORD and devoured them, and they died before the LORD" (Leviticus 10:2). Yet two verses earlier, fire had fallen from God's presence in acceptance of Israel and its worship. It seems the fire that is a blessing when it comes from faithfulness can also be deadly when provoked by disobedience.

When we consider God in the prophets "as a refiner and a purifier of silver," we understand the prophets are not thinking of wrath, but of purifying mercy. As mentioned, in the Bible, fire is symbolic of the intense energy of the divine nature, continually acting upon every person and on everything, according to its nature; here preserving, there destroying; now cleansing, now consuming. The same fire which burns the wood, hay, and stubble, purifies the gold and the silver.

Fire does symbolize the wrath of God in punishing sin, but not in the sacrificial offerings. For instance, the meal offering of Judaism cannot be an atoning sacrifice because no life is offered and no blood is shed even though it is presented daily to God in fire. Furthermore, even in sacrificial blood offerings, the atonement is already fully accomplished, prior to the burning, in the sprinkling of the blood. The fire in this case must mean something other than divine wrath, while still meaning a single thing for all the burnt offerings. The burning which follows the atonement must symbolize the entirety of Jesus' expiatory sufferings.

The burnt offering is the same as that of the meal offering—the ascending of the offering in consecration to God and God's gracious acceptance and appropriation of the offering. We saw it in the first burnt offering at the Tabernacle inauguration when the fire came forth from heaven, lit by no human hand, and was a visible representation of God's acceptance and appropriation of the offering (see Leviticus 9:24). The special meaning of the Old Testament burnt offerings, then, was that complete consecration unto God is essential to right worship. In the burnt offerings, nothing was reserved for the offerer; everything was God's, and in the altar fire, God took the whole in such a way that the offering passed forever beyond the offerer's reach. To the degree the offerer entered into this meaning and his heart corresponded to the outward rite, it was an act of worship.

Whether fully understood at the time or not, every burnt offering pointed to a future Victim, in whose person and work, as the One fully-consecrated Man, the burnt offering would receive its full meaning. Jesus' whole-life sacrifice wrought reconciliation and fellowship through his atoning death, but even that would not have been possible had he not first offered every moment of his life in perfect consecration and entire self-surrender unto God, in perfect obedience.

In his atoning death, Christ died that we might not die, but he did not offer himself in full consecration to God in order to prevent us from offering our own life and death. Instead, he made our self-donation possible in preparation for the Great Feast Day at the Lamb's Supper. Christ himself said in his memorable prayer just before his passion: "For their sake I consecrate myself, that they also may be consecrated in truth" (John 17:19). Paul said the same using the language of burnt offerings: "I appeal to you therefore, brethren, by the mercies of God, to present your bodies as a living sacrifice, holy and acceptable to God, which is your spiritual worship" (Romans 12:1).

The burnt offering, then, teaches us to remember that Christ not only died for our sins, but he also consecrated himself to God for us in total self-surrender. We are, therefore, to plead not only his atoning death, but also the transcendent merit of his life of full consecration to the Father's will. We do this by submitting to the earthly purgatory that consumes our lives as "an offering by fire, a pleasing odor," a fragrant odor, "to the LORD," a burnt offering unto God (see Leviticus 1:9, 13, 17) "which is your spiritual worship," according to St. Paul (Romans 12:1). St. John Henry Newman agrees: "And these two pains, so counter and so keen—the longing for him, when thou seest him not; the shame of self at thought of seeing him—will be thy veriest, sharpest purgatory."[41]

Jesus' total consecration and wholly consumed life bought for us all our blessings and removed all our eternal punishment, and oddly enough, this total holocaust is called his *passion* by the Church.

PASSION AS HANDING ONESELF OVER

As a Lenten discipline, I watch *The Passion of the Christ* every year during the Triduum. It is rough. I have to force myself not to hurry the narrative along (can I use that word for something so violent?), but in my heart, the whole time I just want it to be over.

For several weeks after watching *The Passion,* I find myself praying the Rosary's sorrowful mysteries something like the way I talk myself through difficulty and suffering: *In less than twenty-four hours, it will all be over. Let's just get through this, Jesus. We are in the Garden … Thank goodness, it is morning; you made it; less than nine hours left … OK, now we are carrying that heavy cross. Can you make it up this hill? Just hang on Jesus, we are almost there and then only three hours left …*

To me, although the word "passion" comes from the Latin "to suffer," it has always been a strange word to associate with these long hours of unspeakable acts of torment and agony. Passion is commonly used to denote striving for personal expression. Jesus' suffering is said to be and truly was his passion.

The Bible mostly uses the term "passion" to describe out-of-control emotions and desires (see Galatians 5:24). In Acts, the only use of "passion" is in reference to Jesus' suffering and death: "To them he presented himself alive after his passion" (Acts 1:3). From this mustard seed of a verse sprang a beautiful theological tree in the Church on passion as specific to Jesus' suffering and death.

PASSION IS DELIBERATE VULNERABILITY

If it is possible to enter more deeply into the mystery of holocaust and passion on these terms, I was recently persuaded to do so by Jeannie Ewing's book *Waiting with Purpose.* In her book, she quotes W.H. Vanstone, who invites us to consider passion in another, maybe more challenging, way in his classic book *The Stature of Waiting:*

> The word "passion" does not mean ... "pain": it means dependence, exposure, waiting, being no longer in control of one's own situation, being the object of what is done ... [Jesus] entered into the totality or extremity of passion—the situation in which there is no limit to what may be done to one, to what one may receive or suffer; and at the great climax of the story, at the moment when he is handed over in the Garden, we see him waiting, in the agony of expectancy, for whatever it is that he is to receive.[42]

If Jesus' passion can possibly be more of a stumbling block of salvation (see 1 Corinthians 1:18), I think this does it: leaning into, "passing over" or "passing into," an "agony of expectancy"— patience for an unknown, but deliberate, helplessness at the hands of others.

At the Last Supper table, Jesus' hour for deliberate vulnerability has come. "And he said to them, 'I have earnestly desired to eat this passover with you before I suffer'" (Luke 22:15). As St. Bede comments, "He first then desires to eat the typical Passover, and so to declare the mysteries of his Passion to the world."[43]

A hint of his passion's mystery came later that evening when Jesus said, "All things are now completed." Yet there was something more that was necessary to the completion of Jesus' mission—his passion. He must complete his exodus (see Luke 9:31); he must pass over into the totality of vulnerability in passive waiting; the fire fall of his holocaust is at hand.

Jesus' work on earth was finished. Only after the agony of passive waiting, from the Cross, did he victoriously proclaim, "It is finished" (John 19:30). His final declaration is made in the embrace of extreme, deliberate vulnerability.

WE BEGIN AND END WITH PASSION

Just as striking as his final declaration is his first "declaration." Like us, Jesus was born into total helplessness. He chose this passive vulnerability; he "leaned into" it:

> Though he was in the form of God, [he] did not count equality with God a thing to be grasped, but emptied himself, taking the form of a servant, being born in the likeness of men. And being found in human form he humbled himself and became obedient unto death, even death on a cross (Philippians 2:6-8).

In his helplessness, some will spit on him, beat him, and pierce him; others will marginalize or ignore him entirely. But others will care for him and wash and anoint his battered, broken, lifeless body with great love and tenderness.

Jesus waits in agony of expectation to know: What will I do with him?

WHAT WILL I DO WITH HIM?

Most of what we consider "life" is sandwiched between two periods of inactive helplessness—birth/infancy and death. Passion as dependence straddles human life. Helplessness, then, cannot be inferior to independence.

This punctuation at both ends of my life seems designed to teach, and even warn me, that neither the beginning nor the completion of my life depends on me. Therefore, the value of my lifespan is not solely dependent on the activity, work, or ability to contribute to society that I place so much value on.

So my passion will not necessarily be my doing. Instead, I should consider that it might be the periods where I pass, suddenly or gradually, into a more dependent phase of life. Maybe I am waiting. Maybe I have lost my independence through disability or illness. Maybe I feel or have become what I consider useless or ineffective because I am utterly dependent and can no longer "contribute" or even care for myself.

This is passion the way Jesus teaches it: moving from activity to receptivity, temporarily or permanently. Jesus teaches us that passion seems to depend less on what we express in achieving, and more in what we express in receiving ... *and all of it is redemptive.*

"And what shall I say? 'Father, save me from this hour'? No, for this purpose I have come to this hour." When I allow passion to be something that is done to me rather than what I do, Jesus' passion transforms my waiting, helplessness, and uselessness from a teeth-gritting-count-down-till-it-is-over to the currency of redemption and resurrection.

Human dignity is not diminished in suffering, vulnerability, and helplessness, but accentuated in those who have nothing left to offer when given wholly into God's hands. Passion is a striking corrective to the "do it, fix it" mentality of our times, as the martyrs teach us.

In suffering, in dependence, in helplessness, I am not useless. This does not have to be a sad, unfortunate situation. By grace—and only by grace—I can surrender to the stripping of my attachments and the exposure of my real and raw helplessness.

Like Jesus, I can offer a waiting love that does not try to rush back into or force the action. To Jesus I can offer my presence, gentleness, and mercy. It might be my passing over into this true passion that is the most important and necessary part of my life. Ultimately, as Jesus taught us, this full self-surrender of ourselves as "burnt offerings" in the fire of God's love is the doorway to God's all-consuming love.

LET'S REVIEW

The Catholic Church believes in and teaches the reality of purgatory because:

- Only the perfectly holy are capable of enduring full "sight" of God's essence (see Exodus 33:20; Matthew 5:8).

- Purgatory is the process of purification, or sanctification, that makes us holy and able to bear "seeing" and being one with God and his will.

- Because we are wholly unable to purify our own souls, God himself must perform this purification.

- "Our God is a consuming fire" of love (Hebrews 12:29).

- God's love purifies us.

- Purification is painful because attachments to sin, secret faults, and false perceptions remain hidden in us and cause us to resist God's perfect will.

- God allows trials and temptations in our lives to strengthen virtue, weaken vice, and purify our lives and souls in preparation for union with him.

- Even with God's forgiveness of our sins, without purgatory the smallest actual fault or imperfection would prevent us from receiving our perfectly holy God fully. So purgatory is a great grace.

INVITATION

Part of the duty of Old Testament priests was to participate in bearing the guilt and suffering of the people through the sacrifices they offered on their behalf (see Numbers 18:1). This is also true of our High Priest, Jesus. It is true of us, as well, as members and participants in the common priesthood and the communion of Christ. Sometimes we must "suffer" one another's personalities and differences of opinions. Sometimes we suffer the difficulties of duties in our station in life and the hardships of the present moment. But all of this can contribute to our purification. Let us pray.

God Prompt – LOVE the Word™

LISTEN: "Since therefore Christ suffered in the flesh, arm yourselves with the same thought, for whoever has suffered in the flesh has ceased from sin, so as to live for the rest of the time in the flesh no longer by human passions but by the will of God" (1 Peter 4:1-2).

OBSERVE: Do you offer up your sufferings for the good of your soul and those of others?

What sorts of offerings do you make to God? Are they your first and very best? Your favorite? Are they really a sacrifice for you?

Is God pleased with your offering? How do you know? Spend some time prayerfully reviewing your life and the trials you have faced personally. What are one or two of the most difficult or significant ones?

Identify some ways that you were changed for the better through these trials.

VERBALIZE: Lord, in this time with you, help me identify patterns in the things I have suffered. Could there be something you have repeatedly attempted to teach me through them?

As I think about how fiery trials in my life are an indication of your acceptance of my life as an offering, I feel ...

The knowledge that submitting to trials and sufferings here on earth can ease my purgatory makes me ...

Now that you have worked through this chapter, here is a word of caution, sort of like in Sirach 2:1. There is a distinct possibility that God may offer you what I call a "pop quiz" this week. In this case, it will be a trial that you face. Please do not be surprised. This is not punishment for "doing it wrong." It is God's attempt to help you apply what you are learning and grow in virtue through it. In all probability, it will also not be anywhere near as bad as you might imagine. Right now, before it comes, pray for the eyes to see it when it arrives and to learn the lesson God has hidden in it for you.

ENTRUST: *Lord, help me to be vigilant, to watch and pray. For my adversary, the devil, a roaring lion seeking whomever he may devour (see 1 Peter 5:8), will tempt me to resist and rebel against my trial. Please help me, so that I will not enter into that temptation, for my spirit indeed is willing, but my flesh is weak (see Matthew 26:41).*

Immersed in His Grace

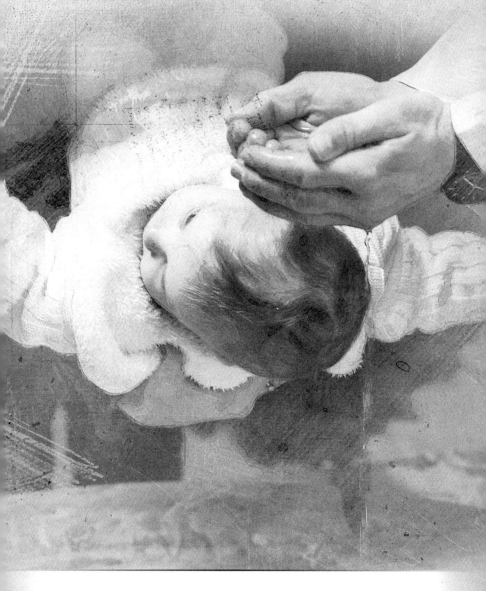

The Laver Is Fulfilled in Baptism

Through the Tabernacle, God communicated himself to the Israelites and called them into his presence. The layout of the Tabernacle taught the people that before anyone is allowed into God's presence, an atoning sacrifice must be offered for his or her sin. But offering sacrifices is a bloody and dirty business, so after the sacrifice was offered, special washing ceremonies were required before the priest could enter the sanctuary.

We have traced the biblical progression of water as a symbol of salvation and refreshment for the people. The Great Flood destroyed and cleansed the earth of its evil and sin, preparing the way for new life in Noah's family. The Red Sea Crossing is interpreted by St. Paul as a type of baptism. The water-rock in the desert provided life-preserving refreshment for the people on their journey through the desert to the Promised Land. According to St. Ambrose, "It was no motionless rock which followed the people."[44] Tertullian agrees, saying, "This is the water which flowed from the rock which accompanied the people."[45] Paul says the rock that followed them through the desert was a type of Christ. It is thought that the water from this rock is what kept the people hydrated and the Tabernacle laver full of water for cleansing.

The prophets continued the theme, using water extensively as a symbol of the New Covenant that revealed how cleansing water would one day also create *new* life. Ezekiel sees a river of life streaming from the right side of the new temple, transforming the land of Canaan to fit it for God's ransomed people to live in. Probably his visions brought to mind the Temple Mount in Jerusalem, where a small stream with "soft-flowing" water actually ran and was regarded in Israel as a symbol of the quiet and unobtrusive influence of the divine Presence there (see Isaiah 8:6). In the New Testament, the shadow of all these Old Testament types is fulfilled.

Today, we hear Ezekiel's prophesies during the Easter Vigil. They were prophetic of the New Testament, in which the living waters of baptism would gush forth in blood and water from the wound in Jesus' side. Jesus told the woman at the well, "Whoever drinks of the water that I shall give him will never thirst; the water that I shall give him will become in him a spring of water welling up to eternal life" (John 4:14). In turn, our sacramental waters of baptism foreshadow the heavenly temple:

> He showed me the river of the water of life, bright as crystal, flowing from the throne of God and of the Lamb through the middle of the street of the city; also, on either side of the river, the tree of life with its twelve kinds of fruit, yielding its fruit each month; and the leaves of the tree were for the healing of the nations (Revelation 22:1-2).

BAPTISM AS SACRAMENT

All these biblical realities reveal the sacramental character of baptism, meaning that the water is an outward symbol that actually brings about the inward reality. Baptism brings about a new creation through the application of Jesus' command to baptize, "in the name of the Father, and of the Son, and of the Holy Spirit."

We saw evidence of this sacramental character when Christ said to Nicodemus, "Unless one is born of water and the Spirit, he cannot enter into the kingdom of God" (John 3:5). Jesus did not necessarily mean one would not be allowed in heaven if he is not baptized, but that one is *unable* to enter heaven for lack of the unique spiritual configuration wrought through baptism that is required to perceive it. Jesus emphasizes his meaning is supernatural, a supernatural rebirth that must be generated by real water and the Holy Spirit, but is literally salvific, as the *Catechism* teaches:

> Through Baptism we are freed from sin and reborn as sons of God; we become members of Christ, are incorporated into the Church and made sharers in her mission: "Baptism is the sacrament of regeneration through water in the word"[46] (CCC 1213).

The Church teaches that there may be extraneous circumstances where baptism is not possible, such as the thief on the cross beside Christ to whom Jesus said he would enter paradise with him. In those cases, it is clear that the person would have been baptized if possible; he or she receives "baptism of desire." The thief on the cross experienced such a baptism.

Additionally, baptism does not mean every baptized person will be saved. Because Scripture teaches that perseverance is required, the Church teaches that the saving grace of baptism can be forfeited through rebellion, complacency, sin, and disbelief. Some born into the Christian faith have little personal connection to it. With the grace imparted by the Holy Spirit during baptism is the inherent expectation that the baptized person will continue in "ongoing conversion" throughout his or her life through the remaining sacraments and personal choices. The Church expects and even requires this to happen: "This is the struggle of *conversion* directed toward holiness and eternal life to which the Lord never ceases to call us"[47] (CCC 1426). Nevertheless, because it is the "gateway to life in the Spirit," the sacrament of baptism is the critical salvation event in a person's life.

We saw the sacramental nature of baptism illustrated in the descent of the Holy Spirit in the dove at Jesus' baptism, when he sanctified our baptismal waters with his presence (see Matthew 3:16). Ephesians 5:26 showed us that it is the water and the words spoken in the Rite of Baptism that accomplish the cleansing. Titus 3:5 clarified that the action of grace performed by the Holy Spirit makes the water and words efficacious. Adding further specificity, Hebrews 10:22-23 includes the baptismal promises, the "confession." We renew this confession every Easter and memorialize it every time we visit a baptismal font and make the Sign of the Cross. If all of this is not enough to convince us of the sacramental character of baptism, St. Peter states outright that baptism now saves us (see 1 Peter 3:20-21).

In biblical times, when a river or other body of water was not located nearby for baptism, people were baptized at the homes of the wealthy or simply by effusion: pouring small amounts of water over the head of the catechumen (much like we do today when we baptize infants). Candidates for baptism entered these baths, which were recessed into the ground, by descending a few steps into water about hip-deep. The bishop poured water over the person's head three times while he knelt in the fetal position to signify the "new birth."

The point is, although the word "baptize" literally means "immerse" or "plunge" in Greek, none of the ancient Christians ever considered a person less baptized if he was not, for some reason, dunked completely into the water. In fact, it was not until about AD 500 that baptism became associated with submersion at all, when the practice of burial above ground gave way to burying the dead underground. At that time, the common understanding of "being buried with Christ" (see Romans 6:4) came to mean "submerged," and baptism by immersion became the norm.

The "laver" also appears in the Catholic Mass. The *lavabo* prayer ("I will wash") in the Mass is derived from the words of Psalm 26:6-12. The priest pours water from the cruet over his fingers into a little dish, then uses a towel to dry his fingers. As he washes his hands, he prays the *lavabo:* "Lord, wash away my iniquity and cleanse me from my sin."

A NEW CREATION

Baptism is the revolutionary seed and configuration, or character of the mark, of the supernatural life. "If any one is in Christ, he is a new creation" (2 Corinthians 5:17). This is an important point, because often we see baptism from a negative perspective, as a taking away of original sin. But baptism also *gives* us something; it incorporates us into the family of God and configures the soul to receive sanctifying grace so that we really and truly share in God's own life.

Committing mortal sin after baptism removes us from the fountain of God's divine life. In effect, we step out from under the continually flowing "faucet" of grace, but the character of the mark of baptism remains. This configuration, by which the soul has been transformed, makes the grace we lost through serious sin easy to recover through confession and repentance: "If we confess our sins, he is faithful and just, and will forgive our sins and cleanse us from all unrighteousness" (1 John 1:9).

While most non-Catholic Christians make no distinction between mortal (serious or grave) and venial (i.e., less serious) sins, the Bible does. In 1 John 5:16-17, we read:

> If any one sees his brother committing what is not a mortal sin, he will ask, and God will give him life for those whose sin is not mortal. There is sin which is mortal ... all wrongdoing is sin, but there is sin which is not mortal.

The Old Testament agrees (see Numbers 15:30-31) as do the Church Fathers. St. Jerome wrote:

> There are venial sins and there are mortal sins. It is one thing to owe ten thousand talents, another to owe but a farthing. We shall have to give an accounting for an idle word no less than for adultery ... There is a great difference between one sin and another.[48]

So, to say that "sin is sin" is similar to saying that a penny and a hundred-dollar bill are both money.

> When you shall have been baptized, keep to a good life in the commandments of God, so that you may preserve your baptism to the very end. I do not tell you that you will live here without sin, but they are venial sins which this life is never without. Baptism was instituted for all sins; for light sins, without which we cannot live, prayer was instituted ... But do not commit those sins on account of which you would have to be separated from the Body of Christ; perish the thought! For those whom you see doing penance have committed crimes, either adultery or some other enormities: that is why they are doing penance. If their sins were light, daily prayer would suffice to blot them out. In the Church, therefore, there are three ways in which sins are forgiven: in Baptism, in prayer, and in the greater humility of penance.[49]

Baptism confers on us the right and ability to receive the other sacraments, particularly the sacrament of reconciliation in the case of mortal sin. If we do not have the "mark" of baptism on our soul, we are unable to receive the sacramental grace of absolution, and our mortal sins would remain unforgiven. This is true of the other sacraments; none of them can communicate grace to us until the capacity for receiving the other sacraments has first been established in the soul by the configuration of baptism. It is through baptism that we "put on Christ" (in the words of St. Paul) and are "configured" to him (in the words of St. Thomas Aquinas). Since there is no escaping the absolute necessity of baptism and no other sacrament is valid without it, the Church insists that babies be baptized as soon as possible after birth. One formally chooses to continue in faith to maturity and apostolate ministry, or not, at confirmation.

What about all those people who die without ever having the chance to be baptized, or maybe never knew about baptism? Will they go to hell through no fault of their own? St. Paul says God gives to every soul he creates sufficient grace to be saved.

> For what can be known about God is plain to them, because God has shown it to them. Ever since the creation of the world his invisible nature, namely, his eternal power and deity, has been clearly perceived in the things that have been made. So they are without excuse (Romans 1:19-20).

And so Pope Francis leads us to pray, "Lord … teach us to contemplate you in the beauty of the universe, for all things speak of you."[50]

WATER TO WINE

After providing the example for baptism in the Jordan River under John the Baptist, Jesus taught mankind its complete meaning. In John 2:2-11, Jesus is at a wedding with his disciples. That it was at a wedding when Jesus performed his first public miracle and inaugurated his public ministry is both an affirmation of the sacrament of matrimony and Jesus' relationship to the Church as the Bridegroom. Jesus' miracle here takes on added significance from the marital context in Ephesians 5:21-33, where Paul says Jesus cleanses his bride, the Church, through self-donation and baptism. Second, you probably already know the water pots here at the wedding in Cana were not our own one or two gallon pitchers, but twenty- to thirty-gallon stone pots used for ritual washings (see John 2:6).

Ritual, Not Moral, Purity

Perhaps it is a good time to note that when reading about Old Testament ritual purifications like those associated with the water pots in Cana, in Leviticus 12–15 for instance, it is important to realize that ritual "uncleanness" in the Old Testament is not the same as moral uncleanness. Contact with corpses and certain physical conditions such as childbirth, for instance, made a person "unclean." But the "uncleanness" extended only to one's fitness to participate in divine worship and to associate with his or her neighbors. Depending on the cause, one's uncleanness lasted longer or shorter amounts of time. Restoration required a ritual cleansing or purification.

A woman's monthly "uncleanness" did not necessarily indicate she was sinful during that time. Similarly, that Uzzah died after touching the Ark does not necessarily illustrate that he went to hell for sin. And for the people as a whole, neither their role as laity nor periods of uncleanness or ritual impurity were considered harmful, inferior, or sinful. Daily life, after all, made uncleanness impossible to avoid, and God knows this. The point was not that one had to be ritually clean at every moment, but that one could not approach God *unless* he or she was clean.

God is willing to live among us, but as he tells us clearly in Isaiah, "For as the heavens are higher than the earth, so are my ways higher than your ways and my thoughts than your thoughts" (Isaiah 55:9). We cannot approach God carelessly or take him for granted. Instead, because God is everywhere, even in our daily, seemingly ordinary lives, holiness and ritual purity teach us that we must take care to keep our lives pure through avoidance of sin and regular confession, so that we can walk at all times with the Lord whose greatness so transcends our ordinariness.

Old Testament ritual purity illustrated the wholly "otherness" of God. He is eternally and utterly transcendent above his creation, so everything related to him must be specially set aside for and configured to him or else be destroyed by his perfection. This unique configuration made any attempt outside of God's prescription to reconcile with him unsuccessful in the same way that software for one printer model will not operate another model, even if they are of the same maker.

Back to the Wedding

There, at the wedding in Cana, under Mary's prompting, Jesus performed his first public miracle by changing the ritual wash water into celebration wine. Jewish and biblical writings, along with Church history, tell us that Mary was taken to the Temple at around age three in fulfillment of her parents' vow of thanksgiving to God for ending the childlessness of their marriage. When still a child herself, Mary's parents consecrated her to God and brought her to the Temple in Jerusalem. She remained there to be educated in preparation by the Holy Spirit for her role as Mother of God, until puberty, at which point she was ritually unclean according to levitical Law and could no longer serve in the Temple.[51]

At that point, as were all cloistered Temple virgins, Mary was assigned to marriage; Joseph would be her new guardian. As she grew into her physical ability to bear a child, her role as mother emerged. Mary necessarily withdrew from the earthly Temple, so she could become the temple of the incarnate Son of God. In celebration of this mystery, both Catholic and Orthodox Churches celebrate a feast day in memorial of the day Mary was presented in the Temple by her parents. The Catholic Church's Liturgy for this feast presents Sirach 24:14-16 as a prophecy for Mary's service at the Temple in Jerusalem.

Just as the Temple virgins prophetically contributed their bronze mirrors to the Tabernacle laver used for ritual washings, Mary, the New Testament Temple Virgin, would contribute to the New Testament "laver." Under her supplication, Jesus' first miracle was to change the water used for ritual cleansing (baptisms) in Judaism—baptisms void of grace or power—into the sacramental new wine of the New Covenant. Wine is a potent scriptural symbol for life, as Jesus will ultimately reveal at the Last Supper, where he shows us the complete fulfillment of what baptism into the New Covenant would ultimately mean.

WASHED IN THE BLOOD

Just before the eve of his supreme sacrifice, Jesus dons the priestly girdle of sacrificial service in the towel he uses to wash the disciples' feet at the Last Supper (see John 13:1-17). The customary Passover ceremony required only a washing of hands, but Jesus added the washing of his apostles' feet. In Mediterranean culture of the time, foot-washing was the duty of menial servants, similar to washing someone's toilet today. Girded with a towel, Jesus washed his disciples' feet, showing them into what sort of baptism they were being "baptized"—a baptism of humility and service.

Stooping in sacrifice as he spoke to them of the importance of baptism for regeneration and confession for ongoing cleanliness, he said, "He who has bathed does not need to wash, except for his feet" (John 13:10). The third-century theologian Origen notes that, "By washing and wiping, [Jesus] made beautiful the feet of those who were to preach glad tidings." Jesus then revealed the crowning glory of baptism: "The cup that I drink you will drink; and with the baptism with which I am baptized, you will be baptized" (Mark 10:39), and he proceeded to walk the terrorizing hill of Golgotha to be crucified. So Jesus' baptism is one of total sacrifice, a sacrifice of his very blood, one that all Christian martyrs share. The washing of feet, however, teaches us that all Christians are called to a "martyrdom" of charity and a total, humble service of others—even if we are not called to suffer a violent or bloody death in his service.

WITH MY BODY I THEE WED

Every Sunday, I saw the man and his wife at Mass. There was nothing remarkable about his appearance. An older man of rather small stature, he sang in the choir, but was otherwise inconspicuous. If it had not been for one marvelous thing, I would have hardly noticed him at all. Characteristic of saints, I hear.

It was a typical Sunday. That morning, in the Rite of Christian Initiation of Adults (RCIA) class I was teaching, we discussed the laver as the second article in the outer court, and its strategic position directly between the altar and the sanctuary entrance; the priests were to wash serving hands and gospel feet in this water after offering sacrifices but before entering the sanctuary in which the Lord presided.

I explained how consistently this is carried forth into Catholic churches where the baptismal font is the first thing one encounters upon entering the sanctuary after a week of sacrifice, just before we enter the holy place to commune with God, and how we memorialize our baptism by making the Sign of the Cross after dipping our hands into the baptismal waters.

We learned that the Tabernacle laver was filled with water from the thirst-quenching rock that followed the Israelites throughout the wilderness, a Rock that St. Paul, in his letter to the Romans, proclaims was Christ (see 1 Corinthians 10:4), so that Jesus was, and is, from where the water and the cleansing proceeds.

I remarked that the baptismal font—the Catholic laver, if you will—is positioned in the church where Jesus' feet would be, and his head at the altar, if one were to imagine the church laid out architecturally like a cross, as most ancient churches were in echo of the cruciform layout of the Tabernacle.

In John 13, we see Jesus, on the eve of his supreme sacrifice, don an Old Testament priestly girdle of sacrificial service (see Exodus 39:29). Girded with a towel, he "lavered" the feet of his disciples, even notorious Judas, showing them into what baptism they were being "baptized."

It is the same baptism into which we are all baptized, that of pure, loving sacrifice, even to death, on the altar of Christ; it is part of what constitutes our spiritual authority and what makes the Church a kingdom of priests, both the ordained and the laity.

With all this from our class jangling about in my head, I headed to Mass that morning. I saw the little man in his usual place at the back *cornu* of the church where the choir sings; I noticed his wife was seated beside him in a wheelchair. She wore full jewelry, bold makeup, and a somewhat fixed stare. I watched him speak softly to her and caress her face as he found the entrance music in the missal and gently fixed her stiff fingers around it before resting it in her lap. He patted her hands. He performs this assistance for her throughout every Mass, between singing with the choir. As always, he was gentle as he sang that morning, leaning over her as though he sang for her, too. He replaced her missal and took a seat beside her against the back wall of the church. At Communion, I saw him struggle to fit the wheelchair between the organ and the aisle; the short way was blocked by oncoming communicants, so he carefully navigated all the way around the back of the pews and down the center aisle so she could receive the Eucharist.

Almost immediately after he retired, this man's wife fell down a flight of stairs and sustained a severe brain injury. While she recovers arduously, the difficulties involved in caring for one who is disabled or handicapped cannot be overstated. When my son had a devastating accident that left him immobile for an extended period, we were discouraged by how the most mundane tasks—dressing, for example—took excruciatingly long to accomplish. Limp, heavy limbs are uncooperative, so that what once took only a minute or two suddenly required an hour to achieve. I wondered how long it had taken the man to bathe his wife, apply her makeup so carefully, choose her Sunday dress, decorate her with earrings and perfume, and place her in the car to meet her Savior. My thoughts returned to the lessons of the morning, and something enormous got in my eye.

I had shared in that morning's class that the ancients did not have access to baths the way we do today. They washed in communal baths, little more than small, shallow pools. Singles bathed in separate baths according to gender, but the old married folk bathed together, and it was the custom for a husband to bathe his wife. With this knowledge and context, St. Paul wrote his beautiful admonition,

> Husbands, love your wives, as Christ loved the church and gave himself up for her, that he might sanctify her, having cleansed her by the washing [laver] of water with the word, that he might present the church to himself in splendor, without spot or wrinkle or any such thing, that she might be holy and without blemish (Ephesians 5:25-27).

Watching that man bathe his wife in sacrificial love, baptizing her in and through his gentle, deliberate care, is one of the most incarnate examples of Christ I have ever witnessed. As a woman and a wife, I know there is no man we respect more than one who sacrifices when it is in our and our children's best interests to do so. I know the inherent authority these sacrifices exert, and that we wives are powerless to resist them. We simply fall at the feet, like the Magdalene, of One who loves us so blatantly.

I know that these sacrifices help women grow as wives and mothers, and they give us the spiritual space to become what God intended us to be, to grow into holiness. This is a husband's privilege as the priest of his domestic church. It is cleansing and powerful, and it is the work of Christ. As his bride, that special man's wife submits in humble charity to the frustration and sufferings to which she seems to have been called. As we saw in our exploration of passion as vulnerability, it is always difficult to submit to God's care through another person, even a husband. I know she feels helpless and weak at his hands, but she looks silently into her husband's intimate gaze, leans into his presence, his gentle touch, the things he whispers in her ear, telling everyone with an eye to see that her submission is also somehow a labor of thankful, tender joy.

Because it is so real, raw, and tender, that man's sacrificial love for his wife, and her submission to it, are together the most stunning illustration of the mystery St. Paul conveys in Ephesians that I have personally ever seen. The glory of it draws me in every week.

Their mutual submission to one another in marriage is an incarnation of the crowning scriptural image of Christ and the Church. Through him, in him, and with him it is our privilege to submit to being bathed, dressed, decorated, and cherished for all eternity, through a sacrifice and cleansing foreshadowed in the Old Testament Tabernacle.

LET'S REVIEW

Christian baptism is a sacrament that initiates salvation because:

- In the Old Testament, God repeatedly used water to save his people to show us how he could use water as a tool of purification and salvation.

- After the atoning sacrifice on the altar, washing in the Tabernacle laver was the next step in preparing to enter the presence of God in the Tabernacle.

- Like Creation, the Great Flood, the Red Sea crossing, and the water-rock in the desert, the Tabernacle laver was a type of baptism.

- When we are baptized, the Holy Spirit descends on us as he did at Jesus' baptism (Luke 3:22).

- Scripture speaks of salvation as a lifelong, ongoing process, not a single point in time.

- Baptism initiates us into the life of Christ and his Church (see John 3).

- The water, with the words and prayers of the Church, accomplish the seed of our salvation (see Ephesians 5:26).

- Scripture tells us baptism now saves us (see 1 Peter 3:21).

INVITATION

The Old Testament laver teaches us that purity is demanded of all those who would approach God. Jesus, our example in all things, is always reminding the Church that baptism brings us into a life of sacrificial love: Like Jesus, we must take up our crosses daily and be crucified with him at the hands of others in love of God and neighbor. Let us pray.

God Prompt – LOVE the Word ™

 LISTEN: "Blessed are the pure in heart, for they shall see God" (Matthew 5:8).

 OBSERVE: Spend a moment or two reflecting in God's presence about areas of your life in which he would like you to pay more attention to purity.

What specific action can you take this week to ensure more purity in this area?

When spending ourselves for others, the weakness of the flesh dictates periods of dryness and loneliness, and our earthly desert sometimes becomes difficult and weary.

Do you have a daily prayer ritual?

How do you draw from the well of Living Water flowing from the stricken rock?

 VERBALIZE: Lord, as I consider the purity you demand of your servants, I am intimidated by ...

I am thankful for your help here ...

I need help here ...

ENTRUST: *Lord, as I consider the purity and sacrifice demanded of your servants, I am intimidated. Help me to show my love for you by sacrificing for others, without thanks, recognition, or even acknowledgment. At the same time, help me thank you from the fountain of love in my heart for all you sacrificed for me and your Church. Help me cooperate with you in my own holiness and that of your people. Amen.*

PART TWO

Drawn into the
Divine Mystery

The Light of Truth

The Lampstand Is Fulfilled in the Magisterium

*J*n exploring the divine design of the outer court of the Old Testament Tabernacle, we discern the overarching theme that God desires to live among his people and be close to them. Through the Tabernacle general, its liturgical year, the priesthood, burnt sacrifices on the bronze altar, perpetual altar fire, and ritual washings in the laver, God draws us into his presence. We are able to appreciate how Jesus fulfilled these Old Testament types in his person.

But Jesus' death, resurrection, and ascension were not the end. Alleluia! He sent the Holy Spirit forward and brought the Old Testament types into the Church, where they will be consummated in the heavenly Jerusalem for even "greater things" (John 14:12). Through the Church, Jesus would not just "tabernacle" among men, as he did in the Old Testament and in the tabernacle of his own body, but tabernacle *in* men, through his body, the Church. The outer court of the Tabernacle was about blood, judgment, death, cleansing, and purification. But now, we are about to enter the inner court, the sanctuary, the Holy Place.

In the sanctuary of the Holy Place, everything is about life, nourishment, light, and the fragrance of incense. It is quiet, silent even. If you think about it, our own churches illustrate this principle. Outside the church, in the world, is where all our weekly personal offerings and sacrifices occur. Then we enter the church lobby, where our conversations, laughter, and fellowship take place. But once we enter the sanctuary, all is still and quiet. The sanctuary lamp flickers, inviting us into its womb of prayer. The thought makes me shiver.

The inner court was a sturdy structure of wooden boards overlaid with gold and covered on the outside with goatskins that protected it from desert wind and sand. The entrance faced east and was protected by a thick, richly embroidered tapestry-like curtain. The sanctuary entrance (the large, inner square) was also covered with a curtain, or veil. Come with me, and let's take a peek inside! We are about to explore in detail how the Tabernacle lampstand prefigured the Magisterium of the Catholic Church.

THE GOLDEN MENORAH

Directly inside the curtain at the entrance of the sanctuary, to the left, was a beautiful instrument used to illuminate it (see Exodus 25:31-40). Depending on the Bible translation you use, it might be called a "candlestick" or "candelabra," but those words are not accurate. "Lampstand" is more precise, because no wax was used. Instead, each branch of the lampstand was topped with a little oil lamp, shaped like a squatty teapot or jinni lamp. Like an almond tree of gold, the lampstand was the most lavishly decorated article in the Tabernacle. It weighed one talent, which was about seventy-five pounds.

Like an eternal flame, the lampstand was required to burn throughout the generations of God's people. Its six branches were beaten out from the central almond stem of the lampstand; each branch was topped with a little bowl-lamp containing olive oil and secured with a light-bearing wick.

Oil is a potent biblical symbol for the Holy Spirit. Priests, prophets, and kings were anointed with oil poured from a ram's horn, which we know is itself symbolic of power and authority. Interestingly, the olive oil was pressed, or "beaten" out (Exodus 27:20), much like our process today. The flesh of the olive does not "bleed" its oil unless pierced or bruised. Perhaps this is why Jesus began his passion on the Mount of *Olives* in the Garden of *Gethsemane* (which means "oil (or olive) press" in Aramaic). As you probably know, the name *Christ* is not a family or personal name but a prophetic title, a Greek form of the word "Messiah," or "anointed one." As the prophet Isaiah foretold regarding the Messiah, "The Spirit of the Lord GOD is upon me, Because the LORD has *anointed* me to bring good tidings to the afflicted" (Isaiah 61:1, emphasis added).

Inside the holy place of the sanctuary, but outside the curtain veiling the Ark of Testimony in the Holy of Holies, the priests were responsible for maintaining the lamps from evening to morning throughout their perpetual generations. They kept the wicks trimmed, the oil topped, and the lamps continuously burning before God. The light from the lampstand flickered against the gold lining and wood-paneled walls of the sanctuary, making the whole room glimmer. Can you imagine how beautiful the golden lampstand must have been in the soft glow of the sanctuary?

This lampstand is the Jewish menorah, and we know from exploring the priesthood that its decoration of almond flowers was symbolic of the light-bearing institutional priesthood. "Light" was a metaphor in Old Testament Judaism for the saving presence of God. The one gold piece used to make the lampstand symbolized the unity of that priesthood, first with God in the Old Covenant, then with Christ himself throughout the New Covenant, as illustrated in Revelation 1:12-20. Jesus is the light-bearing High Priest of the New Covenant priesthood lampstand, anointed with the sevenfold Spirit (see Isaiah 11:1-2), offering continual light to the Church and the world, forever in the heavenly temple.

THE LIGHT OF HIS WORD

The lampstand symbolized that only into the keeping of the priesthood was God's Word for the whole people discerned and communicated through teaching the Law; the oracle in the Holy of Holies; and the "Perfect Lights and Truths," those *Urim* and *Thummim* stones resting in the high priest's breast-pocket. The Jewish historian Josephus says the stones themselves miraculously indicated God's special presence through them so that no one could argue against the word communicated by the priest:

> One of them shined out when God was present at their sacrifices; I mean that which was in the nature of a button on his right shoulder, bright rays darting out thence, and being seen even by those that were most remote; which splendor yet was not before natural to the stone. This has appeared a wonderful thing to such as have not so far indulged themselves in philosophy, as to despise divine revelation.[52]

We also know that when Jesus says, "I am the Light of the World," he is revealing his divinity, given the long Jewish association of God's presence with light. His Word was creative in Genesis 1, when "let there be light" was uttered, and God created physical light. In John 1:1-14, God is creating something new, something spiritual, with his Word. St. John uses two important designations for what will ultimately become, throughout the passage, a vivid description of the Messiah: life and light. The agent of illumination in both the Genesis 1 and John 1 passages is God's Word. God's Word is light.

Interestingly, St. John refers to a now-familiar sacred occurrence in John 1:14 when he says the disciples "beheld his glory, the glory as of the only Son from the Father." This is a specific reference to the *"Shekinah* glory" (from the root "to dwell"), the special name given to the presence of God in the pillar of cloud and fire dwelling in the Tabernacle and guiding them through the wilderness. St. John says the disciples knew the Word of God to be one and the same with the guiding light of God in the *Shekinah.* In the Gospel of John, Jesus is said to be God's presence with us, his teaching Word, and the creative, guiding, saving glory-light that shines in the darkness.

Jesus taught in the synagogues, offering the light of God's Word as a rabbi (see John 6:59; Luke 4:15-30), a title given by the Jews to a doctor (teacher) of the Law, and the people accepted him as such (see Matthew 23:7; John 1:38). Although the title did not come to mean a trained religious professional formally authorized to interpret Jewish Law until after the apostles, even then it was a mark of honor and respect for one who held an office, and the power of Jesus' teaching drew notice and comment (see Matthew 7:28-29). Peter exclaimed, "Rabbi!" when he, James, and John witnessed the divine light emanating from Jesus at the Transfiguration.

All the "lights" of the Old Testament, specifically the Tabernacle lampstand, symbolized the light of God's authoritative presence in his Word through the institutional priesthood. Jesus fulfills them all as High Priest and Word of God who tabernacles with us. By filling the "lights" with the power of salvation, he carries the lampstand forward into the New Testament Church, where Jesus is the center of all the light emanating from the historical, institutional priesthood in the heavenly tabernacle, as we see him in Revelation 1:12-13.

Because God commanded it as part of their duty on his behalf, separating the priesthood from teaching and instruction in the Law would have been unthinkable to the Jewish mind. Certainly, God was not preventing the people from learning, praying, or studying the Law on their own; he was protecting them from doctrinal error and preserving them in unity. The priesthood was *the* office of authoritative judgment for the people, a way of justice for them. The prophets saw that this would be so in the messianic kingdom as well (see Ezekiel 44:23). Can you see how a priestly, magisterial body on matters of faith and doctrine was God's idea? Now as then, they are anointed at ordination with a special discernment charism.

A LIVING HISTORY

Just as Jesus was specially anointed for his role as High Priest, the ministerial priesthood of the Church is specially anointed and configured by the Holy Spirit. Jesus did not come to earth for the solitary purpose of dying on the Cross to atone for our sins. Jesus came also to teach, to demonstrate the "perfect lights and truths" about God that lead us to love him, and to show us how to live in a way that fully experiences and communicates that love.

Jesus returned to heaven at the ascension in his physical, visible presence, but he contrived a way that he could remain with us as our light-bearing teacher until the end of time. Fulfilling the promise in the Old Testament structure, Jesus established his twelve apostles as the pillars of his Church, the foundation of the truth (see 1 Timothy 3:15). Although now through a mystical tabernacle made of living stones, rather than a physical tabernacle in his own body, Jesus remains on earth through the hierarchical structure borrowed from his native Judaism, built on, expanded, and left to us by his apostles.

Jesus himself is the High Priest and head of the new living temple in his body, and the Holy Spirit is its "soul," constantly bringing the Church to a fuller understanding and fulfillment of the public revelation Jesus demonstrated to and taught the apostles. Consequently, there is no "new truth" for us to believe; public revelation, as the Church calls it, ended with Jesus (see Hebrews 1:1-2). Like a flower bud unfolding, or an acorn sprouting and growing into a mighty oak, the deposit of faith continues to flourish under the examination and thought of brilliant minds in every generation.

But early Christian writings prove that the Catholic Church has preserved and believes today exactly what the first Christians believed, the truths they received from Jesus and his apostles. Many of them were written down and compiled in the Bible, but many others were first passed along orally and have been preserved through the living history of the Church's Liturgy, arts, and historical writings. This is why St. Paul says to "stand firm and hold to the traditions which you were taught by us, *either* by word of mouth *or* by letter" (2 Thessalonians 2:15, emphasis added).

When a pope or ecumenical council defines a dogma of the Church, a new truth is not suddenly presented or created from thin air; rather, the new dogmatic proclamation merely confirms and clarifies a belief that was held in the Church from the time of the apostles. Because such a truth was believed by the Church from its very beginning—as proven through her writings, liturgy, and works of sacred art—we must believe it if we are to live in the fullness of the Faith Jesus has given us. Who guards this ancient deposit of faith? The Church, as "the pillar and foundation of truth." Where is Church authority in Christ? The successors of the apostles, the college of bishops. How can we trust them? Jesus says it takes great faith to see God in men (see Luke 7:9). He said to hear them is to hear him (see Luke 10:16). Jesus speaks to us through their special anointing.

A SPECIAL ANOINTING

With each progressive ordination from deacon, to priest, to bishop, the Holy Spirit imparts a fuller configuration that equips him for the mission and authority particular to his hierarchical rank. Like the Old Testament Levites, deacons in the Church today serve Christ's mission and grace by assisting their bishop and parish priests. As did the sons of Aaron in the Old Testament, the Catholic priest is the bishop's (high priest's) subordinate co-worker. He depends on his bishop for the exercise of his authority and is ordained by him to preach the gospel, hear confessions, shepherd the faithful, and celebrate divine worship as a true priest of the New Testament. The full measure of high priestly ordination is reserved for bishops who are prepared for and bear the collective responsibility for the welfare of the whole Church: "Obey your leaders and submit to them; for they are keeping watch over your souls, as men who will have to give account" (Hebrews 13:17). As the levitical hierarchy served God's people through the Old Testament sacrificial system, Catholic hierarchy serves the new people of God through the sacramental economy established by Christ.

The terms "almond," "watch," and "charge" are from the same root and are therefore interrelated in biblical usage. "Watch" and "charge" are used to specify the duty of the priesthood to keep watch over, or guard, the rites and ceremonies *of the altar*—first the altar of the Tabernacle, then through the altar of the Eucharist (see Numbers 3:7-8; Ezekiel 44:15; Hebrews 13:17). In Ezekiel 33, we see the prophet as priest and "watchman," whose duty is to guard the altar and its rites as the most important item in the land, more holy than the land itself. As we have seen, Ezekiel prophesied that the messianic temple, or church, would include a lowered class of "priests" who forfeited the "charge" or "watch" of the altar, and a pure class of priests who "keep watch," or "keep the charge." Only the Catholic priesthood has kept the charge of the altar and its sacraments wholly and unceasingly since Jesus and the apostles. In doing so, they alone have preserved the light of Christ's Eucharistic sacrifice for us throughout history.

Just as the Old Covenant people of God was built on the twelve tribes of Israel, the new people of God under the New Covenant was built on twelve apostles. In fact, it was the "new twelve" that served notice that Jesus was creating a new people of God. Because the whole Church was Catholic until the unholy schism, the Church Fathers, seen here in the words of Tertullian, wrote glowingly about the Catholic Church as the establishment of the apostles: "How blessed is the Church of Rome, on which the apostles poured forth all their doctrine along with their blood."[53]

The *Catechism* teaches: "By virtue, therefore, of the Holy Spirit who has been given to them, bishops have been constituted true and authentic teachers of the faith"[54] (CCC 1558). The pope is a brother bishop and the supreme visible sign of the unity of the Church as its head under Christ. The unity of our college of bishops with the pope constitutes the magisterial, or teaching, authority of Christ on earth. Altogether, they preserve the unity of God's people and the purity of their faith, just as God designed and prefigured in the Old Testament Tabernacle lampstand.

THE CHURCH'S ONE FOUNDATION

Often non-Catholics will dispute the teaching authority of the Church's priesthood with Jesus' command, "But you are not to be called rabbi, for you have one teacher, and you are all brethren" (Matthew 23:8). From this single verse, it may seem as though Jesus does not *want* teaching authority in his Church. Yet Scripture is clear that God personally appoints teachers for his Church (see

1 Corinthians 12:8; Ephesians 4:11). Jesus was making the point the Church itself makes, that the magisterial (from the Latin for "teaching") bishops and priests are servants of God, acting *in persona Christi Capitis* ("in the person of Christ the Head")—that is, with his own authority. The Church does not speak or teach on every issue or on every passage of the Bible. In those areas, we are free to explore with the whole Church. But where the Church does speak and define, Jesus speaks and defines. We must read and study the Bible and contemporary issues with the mind of the Church and live our lives in the heart of the Church if we are to live in and hear God fully.

Hierarchy is not the enemy of God. God loves hierarchy; the angels function in hierarchy; atoms and molecules operate in hierarchy; the plant and animal kingdoms exist in hierarchy; the galaxies rotate in hierarchy in an ordered universe; everything in creation has its role and rank. "But all things should be done decently and in order" (1 Corinthians 14:40). Jesus wants us to know where to find the truth that we can stake our lives on, so he provided us with authoritative interpretation.

If you were going to send someone to the year 4029 in a time machine, would you lead him to the huge, complicated apparatus and say to him, "As my designated time traveler, you are solely responsible for the proper functioning of this time machine. If you operate it correctly, you will arrive safely in the year 4029 and return to your loved ones in the present in one piece. Time travel, though, is delicate and intricate business. If you miscalculate the entrance to a wormhole, press the wrong magnetism allowance, enter the horizon of a black hole, miscalculate the smallest of measurements, or figure a trajectory incorrectly, you and my priceless time machine will be lost forever; you will never see your loved ones again. Here is a book from the future you will be visiting that explains it all. Now go have an adventure!"

You might feel that your life requires more than a book to preserve it, even a book written by future humans who are excited for your visit. A book from the future would be easy to misunderstand. It would probably include future knowledge or idiomatic language that you cannot relate to. You cannot ask the book to clarify its meaning. Suppose a thousand astrophysicists from MIT or CalTech or NASA—or even self-taught, self-appointed astrophysicists— seek to interpret the book's meaning and come up with different interpretations. How confident would you feel about reaching your destination and returning safely?

Leaving aside our time travel metaphor, let's consider the following: Sacred Scripture is thousands of years old. Reliable interpretation for a two-thousand-year-old Church is an absolute, *rational* need that God provided for, in both the Old Testament and the New Testament. Not by putting a book in our hands and leaving each of us to puzzle over it individually as best we can. Just as the Word is a person and not merely a book, the truth comes to us throughout history in Sacred Scripture and the Magisterium. By Jesus' own command and authority, Peter and the other apostles were made the teaching authority of the Church from the very beginning: "He who hears you hears me, and he who rejects you rejects me, and he who rejects me rejects him who sent me" (Luke 10:16). To them Jesus entrusted the fullness of his teachings; through them, Jesus' voice speaks Truth to us, and preserves it in the Church as "the pillar and bulwark of truth" (1 Timothy 3:15). An enormous chunk of the Christian church is completely missing the Eucharist because it separated the Word of God from his institutional priesthood. As the *Catechism* notes:

> It is this Magisterium's task to preserve God's people from deviations and defections and to guarantee them the objective possibility of possessing the true faith without error ... seeing to it that the People of God abides in the truth that liberates (CCC 890).

In speaking to his fellow priests, St. John Paul II exhorted:

> For you I am a bishop, with you I am a priest ... Our task is to serve truth and justice in the dimension of human 'temporality,' but always in a perspective that is the perspective of eternal salvation.[55]

This is what the prophet Malachi meant when he foretold of the messianic priesthood, "For the lips of a priest should guard knowledge, and men should seek instruction from his mouth, for he is the messenger of the LORD of hosts" (Malachi 2:7).

DOES PERFECT MEAN SINLESS?

But mere men are sinful. The divine anointing and perfection of the Catholic priesthood cannot mean that every individual priest is divine or perfect, as you well know. In the same way, the Church as the body of Christ is divinely perfect, but neither you nor I as individual Christians is perfect. The perfection of the institutional priesthood as depicted in the heavenly menorah does mean, however, that by grace and the Holy Spirit, the whole priesthood and the whole Church is greater than the sum of its parts. What do we do, then, when faced with imperfect, flawed, and even gravely sinful priests?

This is a question I first faced as a non-Catholic whose whole spiritual education at God's hands had been on the issue of authority. Authority was the number one issue that propelled me into the Church. I emerged from childhood with profound father wounds that provoked sometimes violent rebellion against authority. My father was aggressive, dominating, and controlling, so I was determined no one would ever force me to do anything I didn't want to do, ever again. You can also understand, then, that I had real suspicions about church authority as well, especially given my experiences in denominational churches.

When I was a twenty-something Baptist church leader, a dispute arose against our pastor. It was nothing more than a personality conflict, really, but I chose a side and had all sorts of opinions that seemed completely righteous and just. After all, he was acting blatantly sinful by attempting to control and manipulate the congregation through the force of his office as pastor, and I could prove it with multiple Bible verses. The problem was, God pointed out my own sin—a critical spirit and sinful gossip—with his Word in my daily Bible reading.

PEOPLE RULE

For instance, in Revelation, St. John writes to seven churches in existence toward the end of the first century. He tells the church at Laodicea that Jesus says he will vomit them out of his mouth for being lukewarm. They are, spiritually, neither hot nor cold. But that is not what got me about the verse. What struck me was that the name *Laodicea* literally means "people rule." The church at Laodicea had stopped listening to God through its leaders, and had become so lukewarm as a result, that they made Jesus sick.

Later, the churches to whom John wrote became representative of eras of Church history, so that the historical Laodicea was prophetic of the Church in the last days, in which people would seek to rule in places where they had no authority. Jesus said this type of rebellion makes him sick because authority is God's and is his instrument for keeping order (see Romans 13:1-3).

So, I asked the Lord what I was supposed to do. Were we supposed to just let the pastor run roughshod over the church, hurt God's people, and turn them away from the faith, possibly to be lost forever? The Lord pointed me to Mary, who quietly obeyed God before a holy man who simply did not yet understand, and whose actions were not those of malice but of not having been drawn fully into the truth at the time she was living it. She assented fully before her family and neighbors, bearing their suspicion. Was Mary a doormat? Was she helpless? Or did she have heroic faith that quietly waited on God to defend her as she prayed in submission to his will?

He pointed me to his prescription for order in Matthew 18:

> If your brother sins against you, go and tell him his fault, between you and him alone. If he listens to you, you have gained your brother. But if he does not listen, take one or two others along with you, that every word may be confirmed by the evidence of two or three witnesses. If he refuses to listen to them, tell it to the church; and if he refuses to listen even to the church, let him be to you as a Gentile and a tax collector (Matthew 18:15-17).

So, I went to the pastor with my complaints, and talked to no one else about them. I did not tell anyone about my discussion with him, in which he became indignant and refused to acknowledge my viewpoint. The Lord then invited me to simply pray for him according to 1 John 5:16, "If any one sees his brother committing what is not a mortal sin, he will ask, and God will give him life for those whose sin is not mortal." Had the Lord not directed me to pray this way, I would have continued in the process of taking another Christian to the pastor and repeating my concern.

A Christian friend and I began a full-on assault on heaven in prayer. I was careful not to gossip, and every time I felt the anxiety of what was happening in our church, I gave it to God again. Nothing happened or changed that I could see. But in six months, that pastor left, and I learned some priceless lessons in proper submission to what I perceived as "bad" authority that I have applied in many other instances through the years: church leaders who thought they owned the place, a pastor who withheld sacraments from those he did not like (he later left the priesthood, entirely), and a seminarian stalker. Sometimes it was necessary to go to a person directly, but most times I just needed to grow up in charity and allow God to work without my interference. Rarely did my direct approach, when I was compelled or led to use it, escape difficult and painful consequences, but I knew to bear them patiently and wait for God to intervene, and he always does.

The Church illustrated this principle beautifully in resisting the inclusion of employer-funded contraception and abortion under the Affordable Care Act. The Church said "no," obeyed God, submitted to the unjust consequences, and waited on God to deliver. Important things are sorted out in the waiting that often have less to do with us and more to do with lessons those "against" us are learning.

St. Teresa of Calcutta (Mother Teresa) said we are infallible when we obey.[56] God never leaves his people helpless. When we do not see God work mightily on our behalf, is it not usually because we are unwilling to submit to mistreatment at the hands of those in proper authority over us and leave the circumstances to him? When we witness injustice and sin, certainly we have a duty to confront it using the prescription he left us and pursue every available avenue of rectification. We must go as far up the leadership ladder as we are able and do the right thing, regardless. The biblical prescription at that point is to bear the consequences to God.

The only time God allows us to disobey authority, which is God-given, is in the case of sin. When an authority commands or wants us to do the wrong things or tries to keep us from doing the right things, we must obey God and trust him with whatever consequences follow. "Whoever knows what is right to do and fails to do it, for him it is sin" (James 4:17).

It was with this verse and Our Lady's example in mind that I came into full communion with the Catholic Church under the censure of my husband, my family, my friends, and my denomination. I did not defend my decision unless asked outright, and I was only asked once. I did not take their condemnation personally because I understood it to be ignorant, and in a backward way, also the hand of God growing me in humility. Their suspicion and judgment was painful—especially my husband's—and clearly in error. But because it was offered from fear rather than malice, I knew to leave the circumstances and convincing to God. In the end, God used a childhood father wound and the resulting rebellion to draw me into the authority of his Church, and my determined submission to him eventually led my husband and family there as well.

I may have already lost you by now, in suggesting God corrects his people's sins through bad leaders (see Romans 13:1-5). After all, we live in times like those of Laodicea, when everyone wants to rule without authority and resist the rule of authority. Obedience would not be an evangelistic counsel if it were easy; indeed, "to obey is better than sacrifice" (1 Samuel 15:22), powerful *because* it is so sacrificial. If you are a simple soul like Our Lady, you will know God "poured forth wisdom" (Sirach 50:27) from his heart in teaching us to submit to him through our leaders—without compromising with sin, of course.

Through our priesthood, Catholics maintain God's design for unity and trustworthy, authoritative interpretation and teachings of the deposit of faith, given once for all by Christ. They have rested in the guardianship of our teaching priesthood, the Magisterium of the Church, for two thousand years.

Non-Catholic Christians did away with seven books of the Bible and God's design completely when they split from the Church around AD 1500, at which point doctrine and interpretation of Scripture became a matter of division and personal interpretation. But Scripture itself forbids both denominationalism and private interpretation of

Scripture (see 1 Corinthians 3:1-9, 21-23; 2 Peter 1:20) because they lead to disunity and error.

> The Magisterium is not superior to the Word of God, but is its servant. It teaches only what has been handed on to it. At the divine command and with the help of the Holy Spirit, it listens to this devotedly, guards it with dedication, and expounds it faithfully. All that it proposes for belief as being divinely revealed is drawn from this single deposit of faith.[57]

LET'S REVIEW

The Catholic Magisterium has the authority and duty to teach and guard the Word of God and all that is worthy of belief because:

- Throughout the Old Testament, God communicated that authoritative light comes from his presence and his Word through the priesthood.

- The golden menorah was the only light source in the sanctuary.

- The decorative almond blossoms and branches on the Tabernacle lampstand were symbolic of the institutional priesthood in God's presence.

- Jesus is the Word of God, depicted in the heavenly temple as present at the center of the priesthood throughout Church history.

- Even when the priesthood is marred by faithlessness, God is faithful, for he cannot deny himself (see 2 Timothy 2:13).

- Scripture shows us that, through Christ, the magisterial priesthood interprets Scripture and speaks on faith and morals with God's authority.

- The Catholic Church is the only church on earth with both an apostolic and magisterial priesthood.

INVITATION

In Jewish thought and in the Old and New Testaments, God's Word is synonymous with his presence, his light, and his priesthood. Therefore, it is God's presence in his Word, through his priesthood, that brings light. The individual Christian's responsibility to read and study the Bible for himself must take place under the Magisterium of the Church if the Bible is to be learned and practiced without error. Just as the seven lampstands surrounding Jesus in the heavenly temple (see Revelation 1:12-13) depict Jesus at the center of the institutional, Catholic priesthood, the same seven lampstands radiating outwardly from the Light of the World depict the whole of the historical Church, led by the episcopacy, as the sacred illumination of the world. Let us pray.

God Prompt – LOVE the Word ™

 LISTEN: "Obey your leaders and submit to them; for they are keeping watch over your souls, as men who will have to give account" (Hebrews 13:17).

 OBSERVE: Pray and ask God to identify one or more statements or passages from Scripture from this chapter that he wants you to understand, memorize, or practice. Perhaps you would like to underline it (or them).

In your life and circumstances, where do you need more light from God?

Do you want him to order and bring purpose to your circumstances? Do you want his light?

What will this require of you?

VERBALIZE: Lord, the most meaningful statement or Bible passage through which you spoke to me in this chapter was ...

Lord, I believe that in response to my reading in this chapter, you want me to ...

As I think about my problem, challenge, or circumstance, I need your light here ...

When I think about what your light might reveal to me about my circumstances, I feel ...

I need your help to ...

 ENTRUST: *Lord, I believe. Help my unbelief! Amen.*

The Bread of Life

The Presence Bread Is Fulfilled in the Eucharist

*R*emembering that the fulfillment of an antitype must in all ways be better than its promise in the type, it is impossible that Jesus could have been speaking figuratively in John 6 when he said, "he who eats my flesh and drinks my blood lives forever." The term "Presence Bread" as Old Testament type foreshadows Jesus' actual, supernatural presence in the New Testament fulfillment of the Eucharist.

Throughout their history, God prepared the Israelites for the promise of the New Covenant in Jesus' Body and Blood through the particular significance of bread and wine offerings, by foreshadowing the Eucharist in the symbolism of the Tabernacle Presence Bread. Even for the Israelites, the word "shewbread" meant Bread of the Face or Presence. Who else is the Face of God but Christ? To this day, matzo bread carries great symbolism: it is flat with lines and holes in it. Just as the Bible says, the Messiah was pierced and wounded, and by his stripes, we are healed (see Psalm 22:16).

Add to that the first priest's offering, Melchizedek's bread and wine; the Passover lamb with bread and wine; the morning and evening sacrifices on the altar with incense, bread, and wine; the covenant inauguration sacrifice and meal with bread and wine; the daily manna in the wilderness, a pot of which was preserved forever in the Ark of the Covenant with the priesthood and the Law; the twelve loaves of the Bread of the Face in the Tabernacle with bread and wine; all of these witness poetically to us for generations of God's promise of spiritual nourishment to come in Christ through bread and wine. For this reason, theologians tell us that typology is the spirit of prophecy.

Now, promise is swallowed up in event. The blueprint is filled full to overflowing. The Old Testament economy of shadows has given way to the New Testament sacramental economy. The Eucharist has come. The New Covenant is present in his Eucharistic person. Alleluia!

Because the Eucharist is so central to Christianity as to be a matter of life and death, and the Catholic Church teaches what the apostles originally understood and taught about the Eucharist, we are going to spend some time looking at the early Church's understanding and treatment of the Eucharist. Let's begin in the Gospels.

IT IS THE LORD!

On the road to Emmaus, Jesus explained himself to the grieving disciples through the prophetic typology, but they *did not discern him in his word*, even though their "hearts burned" with the truth of it all pouring from his sacred lips. Instead, when they asked him to abide with them, he answered their request by "staying" with them in the Eucharist. Not until the "breaking of bread" did they recognize his presence with them (see Luke 24:13-35).

Did he disappear as soon as they recognized him because they no longer needed his personal, physical body? Could his earthly body, in fact, have been an impediment to his *fuller* presence in the Eucharist, upon which we are to eat unto eternal life?

In the years leading up to my full communion with the Church, I remember praying a prayer similar to that of the disciples on the road to Emmaus. I prayed, "Lord, I just want to be *closer* to you. Is there not some way we can be closer?" I truly longed to the point of almost desperation for a closer closeness. I thought it was impossible. And then he led me to his Church, where he gave himself to me in the Eucharist. What an incredible miracle, one I do not take for granted. It is the Lord, indeed.

IT IS THE SPIRIT

Recall also his words, "It is the spirit that gives life, the flesh is of no avail" (John 6:63). Did he mean there is no profit in his own flesh, the broken and spilled out flesh and blood of the New Covenant? Was he saying he merely spoke in symbols?

How could that be his meaning after he made it plain that eating (*masticating* in Greek) and drinking his Body and Blood is to eat and drink unto eternal life? Or did he mean we cannot understand his teaching in a human sense, as though he spoke of cutting of the flesh of the Word into pieces and distributing the bloody bits to all who would believe? This is what some disciples thought, and given the prohibition in the Law against eating blood (see Leviticus 17:11), they took offense at him. But the levitical prohibition was given in order that it should point to the promise to come; animal blood cannot convey eternal life, but the divine flesh and blood of the Lamb, separated on the Cross but offered to us, can and does.

Please understand that the "spirituality" of a teaching does not make it symbolic. To be spiritual does not necessitate a "symbolic" meaning. "Spiritual" never means "symbolic" in Scripture; it always means "super- or hyper-natural." In fact, perceiving how literally Jesus was speaking, many true disciples ceased to follow him, but it was spoken as a statement of absolute fact: Eternal life is only in Christ; when one eats his eternal flesh and drinks his eternal blood, one has eternal life.

Despite this assurance, "some did not believe," and Jesus claimed that they, in fact, could not believe what the Catholic Church teaches, that Jesus is present in the Eucharistic Bread of the Presence, feeding us with himself in scandalous humility, *unless* the Holy Spirit illumined them. It is this section of the Bible in which the Church Fathers put forth that Judas turned definitively away from Christ and toward betrayal (see John 6:66).

Trying to explain his words, "You must eat my flesh," as a figure of speech is also woefully inadequate. Among the Jews (to whom Jesus was speaking), whenever the phrase "to eat someone's flesh" was used figuratively, it meant to hate that person or to take revenge against him. Similarly, to "drink someone's blood" meant to torture him. Neither of the figurative meanings would have made sense as Jesus' meaning.

The apostles took, "This is my body," and, "This is my blood," literally and preached this mysterious doctrine to the infant Church. Jesus would hardly have allowed himself to be misunderstood in the seriousness of the Last Supper, immediately before the Passion; figurative language would have been completely inappropriate. Jesus' true, literal presence in the Eucharist was the universal belief of all Christians for a thousand years, until a heretic named Berengarius in the eleventh century taught the figurative interpretation. His teaching was condemned by three Church councils as heresy, and eventually he retracted his teaching and returned to communion.

The apostles' teaching remained unmolested until Martin Luther, who wanted to abolish the priesthood and therefore rejected the doctrine of the Eucharist as the true and substantial presence of Christ, a doctrine taught by the apostles and firmly believed by all Christians for 1500 years. Jesus could hardly have been more emphatic: "My flesh is food indeed, and my blood is drink indeed" (John 6:55). Either Jesus lied, or he allowed a misunderstanding that amounts to idolatry in the earliest Church that has led us Catholics to worship a piece of bread for two thousand years. The idea of Jesus speaking in metaphors at the Last Supper is even more cruel when we remember he was addressing men who were mostly poor fishermen, uneducated in the niceties of rhetoric.

We know the apostles and early Church understood Jesus literally, in part because of the way they spoke of the Eucharist in Scripture. St. Paul says he hands on the Eucharistic teaching wholly, as it was given to him:

> For as often as you eat this bread and drink the cup, you proclaim the Lord's death until he comes. Whoever, therefore, eats the bread or drinks the cup of the Lord in an unworthy manner will be guilty of profaning the body and blood of the Lord. Let a man examine himself, and so eat of the bread and drink of the cup. For any one who eats and drinks without discerning the body eats and drinks judgment upon himself (1 Corinthians 11:26-29).

One could hardly be guilty of the Body and Blood of the Lord, or bring judgment (literally, damnation) upon himself, were his Body and Blood not truly present, or if the bread he ate were merely bread, even blessed bread, and if the wine was just wine, even prayed-over wine.

Just as the Old Testament Tabernacle was Presence and sacrifice, the New Testament tabernacle, Christ's body, is both presence and sacrifice. Brant Pitre tells of the Jewish custom in which the priests lifted the Table of Presence Bread in procession throughout the congregation, proclaiming, "Behold God's love for you!" How much more, now, the real presence of God's love in Christ, our living Presence Bread? How can we not fall down in worship as he reigns in the monstrance?

All accounts of the Last Supper say that on the night he was betrayed, Jesus took bread and wine into his sacred hands and "gave thanks." Ann Voskamp says if Jesus can give thanks in being betrayed, so can we. And so, from the Greek word *eucharistia,* which means "a giving of thanks," we get the name of our sacrament, the Holy Eucharist.

Because he offers his own Body and Blood, the Eucharist is both sacrifice and sacrament. As *the* New Testament sacrifice, the Holy Eucharist is the Mass, or the New Covenant. In the Mass, God works through the priest, who prays Christ's own words directly over the bread and wine, changing them into his own Body and Blood for us: "This is my body." Notice all that is contained in this tiny sentence, by emphasizing each word in turn:

"*This* is my body, given up for you."

"This *is* my body, given up for you."

"This is *my* body, given up for you."

"This is my *body,* given up for you."

"This is my body, *given* up for you."

"This is my body, given *up* for you."

"This is my body, given up *for* you."

"This is my body, given up for *you.*"

Jesus is not present in the Eucharist in miniature. He is there in the fullness of his resurrected, glorified person, but in a supernatural way that suspends the laws of space and time. His Body and Blood have no weight or height or breadth or thickness, because he is present in a supernatural way. He does not multiply himself into many different Jesuses or divide himself into as many pieces as there are hosts. There is one Jesus, whole and undivided. To deny that is to be a heretic, according to the early Church.

St. Ignatius of Antioch, a disciple of St. John, equated prayer and the Eucharist, just as the Church does today:

> Take note of those who hold heterodox opinions on the grace of Jesus Christ which has come to us ... They abstain from the Eucharist and from prayer because they do not confess that the Eucharist is the flesh of our Savior Jesus Christ, flesh which suffered for our sins and which that Father, in his goodness, raised up again. They who deny the gift of God are perishing in their disputes."[58]

Pope Benedict XVI wrote:

> The Eucharistic Celebration is the greatest and highest act of prayer, and constitutes the centre and the source from which even the other forms receive "nourishment": the Liturgy of the Hours, Eucharistic adoration, *lectio divina,* the Holy Rosary, meditation. All these expressions of prayer, which have their centre in the Eucharist, fulfil the words of Jesus in the priest's day and in all his life: "I am the good shepherd; I know my own and my own know me, as the Father knows me and I know the Father; and I lay down my life for the sheep" (John 10:14-15).[59]

In the Eucharist, we are all gathered into one through him, in him, and with him, as the word "communion" illustrates: *with union.* Some of the earliest prayers of the Mass, recorded in the *Didache,* illustrate this understanding: "As this broken bread was scattered over the hills [as grain], and was gathered together and became one, so let your Church be gathered together."[60]

As long as the "appearances" of bread and wine remain, Jesus is present with us. Once the "appearances" of bread and wine are digested, Jesus is no longer sacramentally present, but his grace remains.

At Jesus' word and direction, the Mass continues the one sacrifice of Christ through time and makes it present at each celebration as

Jesus commanded: "Do this in remembrance of me" (Luke 22:19). You can see, then, that with these words, Jesus made his apostles priests. Jesus' words *are* the Mass; they are the New Covenant—the sacred action by which Jesus makes himself and his passion present under the appearances of bread and wine.

IT IS THE MASS

From the Last Supper accounts, where Jesus "took bread, and when he had given thanks he broke it and gave it to them" (Luke 22:19), the early Christians called the Mass "Giving of Thanks," "Breaking of Bread," and the *"Agape* (or Love) Feast." Acts 2:42 tells us: "And they devoted themselves to the apostles' teaching and fellowship, to the breaking of bread and the prayers." The breaking of bread and the prayers is the early Mass.

Because the first Christians were Jews, they did not realize at first how completely their break with Judaism would be in Christ. They continued to attend and take part in the synagogue prayers and liturgy until they were excommunicated and persecuted, and finally the Temple was destroyed by God's providence in AD 70. "And day by day, attending the temple together and breaking bread in their homes" (Acts 2:46), they met privately for the "Breaking of Bread" until they were expelled from the synagogues by their fellow Jews who felt they were hijacking the Jewish faith. At that time, the "Breaking of Bread" service began with a prayer service modeled on the synagogue that included two readings (one from the Law and one from the Prophets), followed by a sermon or homily, with prayers interspersed between. Already you can plainly see the Liturgy of the Word, followed by the Liturgy of the Eucharist—the Mass.

This order of worship, this Liturgy, was established as early as AD 150, as we see from the writings of St. Justin Martyr,[61] who says plainly:

> For not as common bread nor common drink do we receive these
> ... as we have been taught, the food which has been made into the
> Eucharist by the Eucharistic prayer set down by him, and by the
> change of which our blood and flesh is nurtured, is both the flesh and
> the blood of that incarnated Jesus.[62]

After the "Breaking of Bread" ceremony was separated from the
Agape Feast and the readings and prayers were added in the style
of the synagogue model, the word "Mass," meaning "going forth" in
Latin, was used to designate the Eucharistic Liturgy upon which
the New Covenant and the Christian Faith was founded. Not as a
mere preparatory ceremony that made Communion possible, the
Church's understanding of the Mass was threefold: a memorial, a
holy banquet, and a sacrifice.

A Memorial

The *Catechism of the Catholic Church* describes the meaning of the
Eucharist as memorial:

> The Eucharist is the memorial of Christ's Passover, that is, of the
> work of salvation accomplished by the life, death, and resurrection
> of Christ ... It is Christ himself, the eternal high priest of the New
> Covenant who, acting through the ministry of the priests, offers the
> Eucharistic sacrifice. And it is the same Christ, really present under
> the species of bread and wine, who is the offering of the Eucharistic
> sacrifice (CCC 1409–1410).

"The cup of blessing which we bless, is it not a *participation* in the
blood of Christ? The bread which we break, is it not a *participation*
in the body of Christ?" (1 Corinthians 10:16, emphasis added).
Remembering that a memorial in Jewish understanding is a re-
participation, or re-presentation, Jesus is not simply asking me to
recall his cross and resurrection with quaint poignancy, but to *receive*
him in the Mass—Body, Blood, Soul, and Divinity—in an unbloody,
sacramental, but truly real way. As a participation in Jesus' Body and

Blood, the merits and graces of his sacrifice are applied directly to my needy soul and enable me to "go forth" to also be broken and spilled out for others in love of him. The last sentence of the Mass is, "Go forth the Mass has ended."

A Covenant Meal

Like the covenant meal shared by the Israelites at the foot of Mount Sinai upon the ratification of the Old Testament, our Mass is a sacred covenant banquet. Originally, the first Christians followed Jesus' example at the Last Supper and celebrated the Eucharist as part of an actual banquet. Gathering in a member's home since there were no churches yet, each member brought food and wine according to his means, and it was shared by all as an act of love *(agape,* meaning "sacrificial love") for one another. At the conclusion of the meal, the bishop celebrated the Eucharist after the example of Christ. But almost right away, the *agape* fellowship meal was separated from the sacred Eucharistic celebration in order to preserve its solemnity, due to abuses. St. Paul left such an account for us in First Corinthians, where he scolded the wealthier Christians for consuming their own food and drink without regard to the poorer and even drinking to excess at the *agape* meal (see 1 Corinthians 11:20-22).

The Mass is a participation in Jesus' life-giving presence, and it is a divine banquet in his own flesh and blood that feeds the soul unto the unity of eternal life. But perhaps most importantly, the Mass is a sacrifice.

A Sacrifice

Although now we typically associate the word "sacrifice" with something painful and distasteful that we must leave off or do, the original meaning of sacrifice was tied directly to the priest, who offered a group sacrifice to God for group worship. The Eucharist is a true sacrifice in the strictest sense of the word: It is the offering of a worship-gift to God on behalf of a group, of which its complete destruction indicates that it is a gift to him by a person with the right to represent the group. But Jesus' sacrifice is an eternal sacrifice, so each Mass is not a re-crucifixion in which Jesus dies as victim over and over, but a continuation or prolongation in time of the original sacrifice of Jesus as both Priest and Victim.

There is no time and space in God; there is no yesterday or next millennium for him. In the mind of God, Jesus is both eternally sacrificed and resurrected, *at the same time:* "I saw a Lamb standing, as though it had been slain" (Revelation 5:6). At Mass, you and I are drawn into the single "moment" that is God. Time and distance are swallowed up into eternity in a mystical sense, so that you and I are present at the Cross with all the saints and angels as Jesus sacrifices his Body and Blood for us.

> "Do this in remembrance of me." We carry out this command of the Lord by celebrating the *memorial of his sacrifice.* In so doing, *we offer to the Father* what he has himself given us: the gifts of his creation, bread and wine which, by the power of the Holy Spirit and by the words of Christ, have become the body and blood of Christ. Christ is thus really and mysteriously made *present* (CCC 1356–1357).

In teaching that the Eucharist is the greatest of all sacraments, perhaps it seems we state the obvious. Baptism is, of course, the most necessary sacrament, since it is the gateway to the other sacraments (see John 3:3). Yet, despite all the wonderful things that baptism and the other five sacraments accomplish in the soul, they are still mere instruments of God for the giving of grace, whereas in the Eucharist, we have not only the instrument for giving of grace— we have the actual Giver of grace himself, Jesus Christ, our Lord, the true and final Presence Bread.

LET'S REVIEW

The Presence Bread is fulfilled in the Eucharist because:

- Through numerous Old Testament types, especially the miraculous daily manna and Presence Bread in the Tabernacle, God prepared his people for the Presence Bread of Life in Christ offered daily for the Church.

- In order to be a true antitype, a thing must be in all ways greater; therefore, none of the New Testament fulfillments of Old Testament bread can be merely physical or simply symbolic. The Lord's Supper must communicate grace and therefore eternal life.

- Jesus said the Eucharist is supernatural bread, not symbolic bread.

- Receiving the Eucharist is a participation in the Body and Blood of Christ (see 1 Corinthians 10:16) and therefore real and true, eternal Presence Bread.

- Receiving the Eucharist unworthily makes one "guilty of profaning the body and blood of the Lord" (1 Corinthians 11:27).

- Because Jesus' flesh and blood are resurrected and alive, he stipulated that we must eat his flesh and drink his blood or we cannot also have eternal life (see John 6:53-58).

- The Catholic Church has wholly maintained Jesus' teaching on his real presence in the Eucharist since the apostles.

INVITATION

The Catholic Church has wholly maintained Jesus' teaching on his real presence in the Eucharist since the apostles. Other Christian churches watered down the purity of the Scripture teaching or abandoned it entirely in designating it a mere symbol. Our Holy Eucharist is in the presence of God through Christ, but also *is* eternally the presence of God, tabernacling with us in, with, and through Christ in his Church. The Eucharist is the consistent continuation of God's command that there be perpetual Bread of the Presence in the Tabernacle. Let us pray.

God Prompt, LOVE the Word ™

LISTEN: "Give us this day our daily bread" (Matthew 6:11).

OBSERVE: How does God's daily provision of bread for his people in the wilderness make you more confident of his provision for you today in your life and circumstance?

Have you ever experienced a drastic change in financial circumstances? Have you ever been "hungry"?

What, if anything, did you learn through that experience?

When have you been spiritually hungry?

What assurance can you have after this chapter, about God satisfying that hunger?

Pray and ask God to identify one or more statements or Bible passages from this chapter that he wants you to understand, memorize, or practice. Perhaps you would like to underline it (or them).

VERBALIZE: Lord, the most meaningful statement or Bible passage through which you spoke to me in this chapter was ...

Lord, my biggest hang-up about the Eucharist is ...

I believe that in response to my reading in this chapter, you want me to ...

As I think about my problem, challenge, or circumstance, I need your provision here ...

When I think about the care with which you provide for your people, I feel ...

I need your help to ...

 ENTRUST: *Lord, I believe it is your desire to feed all my hungers. Thank you for being present with me through the Eucharist. Thank you for feeding me with the bread and wine of your Body and Blood. I am not worthy that you should enter under my roof, but only say the word and my soul shall be healed. Amen.*

Holy Smoke

Incense Is Fulfilled in Prayer

One of the most glorious details of the Catholic Liturgy to me when I was a non-Catholic, was the use of incense. Oddly enough, the first time I was present at a Liturgy that included it, I was completely shocked by the fact that it actually smelled! I had seen a news story once on a papal Mass in an Italian cathedral, during which the censer was so enormous, a group of priests was required to swing it from the towering rafters like a pendulum. As I watched smoke pour out of its filigreed holes upon each swing back and forth in front of the altar, it simply never occurred to me that a smell must be permeating the whole cathedral.

But that changed the night of my first Mass, an Easter Vigil Mass at which a friend was entering full communion with the Church. I thought it was the weirdest thing I had ever witnessed. I had no idea what all the standing and kneeling and bowing and other rituals meant, so as an outsider, the incense was particularly captivating because I completely understood the biblical meaning behind it. I watched the priest process down the aisle behind plumes of smoke billowing from the little censer, saw it waft leisurely up into the rafters and eaves of the church, and creep toward us sitting in the pews. And then, suddenly the scent of it hit me like a wall of glory, and tears welled up with the beauty of it. How silly that I had not expected to smell something. Immediately, I remembered that televised cathedral Mass with awe, realizing the whole place must have been covered in scent, as I was that moment. What a wonder!

After that Mass, I found the nearest Catholic store and, under cover of night, I bought a can of Lebanon Cedar liturgical incense and snuck it home like it was contraband. It was the first Catholic purchase I ever made. Because I was non-Catholic at the time, I scandalized my denomination by adding what they considered this New Age hooey to my Bible study classes. To this day, incense always reminds me of the "Holy Ghost," and I shiver like that first time at the sense of "holy ghostliness" I felt watching the smoke rise and dissipate. Whose idea was it to combine liturgy, incense, and prayer? It was God's!

HOLY SMOKE

Nestled in the quiet glow of the Holy Place, just beyond the golden lampstand and the Table of Presence Bread, rested the golden incense altar. Like the Table of Presence Bread, the incense altar had a golden crown decorating the top, signifying that our prayers are crowned. About eighteen inches square and three feet high, this mini-altar was a stand used to burn incense in the sanctuary. As with the Ark of the Covenant, the Table of Presence Bread, and the bronze altar, the incense altar was made of acacia, a wood similar to cedar. But unlike the bronze altar, it was overlaid with gold: bronze for judgment, gold for divinity. Somehow prayer is crowned with divinity in originating from his presence, and ascending to his presence, as our Liturgy teaches us, "Grant us the petitions you inspire us to ask."

As with other instruments in the Tabernacle, rings and poles were used for convenient portability when the Israelites traveled through the wilderness. Like the bronze altar, the incense altar included horns at each corner, signifying the potency and authority of sacrificial prayer. However earnest and pure the breathing of the soul to God may seem, something unworthy mingles with what is best in man, so the altar of incense also had to be cleansed once a year throughout the generations. The horns on both sacrificial altars were purified from the sins of the Israelites with the blood of atonement, revealing the necessity of purifying both sacrifices and prayer of mixed motives and disordered desires, as St. James points out in his teaching on prayer: "You ask and do not receive, because you ask wrongly, to spend it on your passions" (James 4:3).

A special formula of sweet incense was to be burnt daily upon the golden altar with the offering of every daily sacrifice—morning and evening—and left burning continually throughout the day and night as a pleasing aroma to God. A continual cloud of smoke filled the inner chamber, particularly at the moment when the sacrificial blood was sprinkled around the great bronze altar outside.

INCENSE IS YOUR WORSHIP BREATHING

Perhaps nothing in the Tabernacle communicates the holiness of the physical senses like incense. Water purifies, light lets us see, bread nourishes—all necessary in the normal way of life. But incense? It seems so superfluous, yet divinely so.

I think it is because God wants us to know the senses *matter* in worship. If to love God with all your heart, soul, mind, and strength is the essence of the first commandment, then surely every sense must be necessary to do so. After all, mountain breath swirls in mists of earth, fir, and pine; the restless ocean spits in salty foam and spray; dewy flora, steamy fauna, raindrop drizzle, hoarfrost; it all aspirates. Isn't nature's breath the subtlest fragrance and the most impalpable existence known to sense? So "holy ghostly."

Science tells us the olfactory sense is the strongest for triggering memory because the smell-analyzing region in the brain is closely connected to regions that handle memory and emotion.[63] A stray whiff of burning leaves; clear wrapping tape; lake water; or funnel cakes, and suddenly you are transported back in time, immersed in a flood of vivid memories, usually connected to childhood. It all seems to be teaching us that scent is matter passing into the immaterial, the sigh of the senses for the spiritual state of being. In worship, fragrance is spiritual aspiration.

Incense is your worship breathing.

Surely this is the wisdom behind God's accommodation of the sense of smell in worship by providing a dedicated altar for incense burning. Smaller than that for burnt offerings, but much more precious, the incense altar was plated all around and crowned on top with gold. The ingredients for liturgical incense were the best and rarest of their kind, and artisanship was necessary for its preparation.

TO OBEY IS BETTER THAN TO SACRIFICE

Perhaps to preserve the strength of the memories associated with its scent, God commanded that the incense and its formula were sacred and set apart exclusively for Tabernacle use, never to be made or used for common purposes on pain of excommunication or death (see Exodus 30:37-38). Like Miriam, King Uzziah developed leprosy after his pride against the priestly consecration that preserved the sacredness of the Tabernacle, its furnishings, and practices. Ignoring

192 | *Fulfilled: Uncovering the Biblical Foundations of Catholicism*

the strict limits placed on his access to the Temple and role in worship, King Uzziah walked into the Temple with a censer presuming to burn incense there, a duty reserved for Aaron's descendants (see 2 Chronicles 26:16-21). Remember that leprosy was a visible sign of ritual uncleanness that separated one from service and the Tabernacle completely. Unlike Miriam, for whom Moses and Aaron interceded and God removed her leprosy, Uzziah was separated from the Temple for the rest of his life and died with leprosy.

As we have considered many times throughout our study, it is useful to remind ourselves that such strict punishments over seemingly minute infractions were necessary in the Old Testament to preserve the purity of type throughout all those millennia. The Tabernacle sanctuary was a type of God's presence; fire is a biblical type of God; incense is a biblical type of prayer. King Uzziah is a type of presumptuous "worshiper" who makes a show of strutting into God's presence however and whenever he pleases, full of sin and no intention of remedy, tossing out demands or silly, selfish pleas that originate from his pride in what he thinks he deserves rather than from a desire for what is best, humble, or holy. That Uzziah's leprosy appeared and remained on his forehead, the seat of intelligence, for all to see, indicates that his sin was pride and presumption. Apparently, he assumed his way of worship was the better way, rather than the humility and holiness of obedience that God has asked for and deserves.

The incense altar was closest to God's presence in the Tabernacle, centered in front of the mercy seat on which the cloud rested directly behind the curtain, indicating that prayer leads directly into his presence when nothing else can, "for, 'every one who calls upon the name of the Lord will be saved'" (Romans 10:13). Precious, fragrant spices, the purest and most potent, were kindled there before the veil with coals taken from the great altar fire that originated with God and burned perpetually (see Leviticus 6:8-13). No "strange" incense could be offered, only what was prescribed by God; mixing prayer with any human, self-asserting, intrusive element, is "unholy incense" (Exodus 30:9), since *"humility* is the foundation of prayer" (CCC 2559).

A HOUSE OF PRAYER

Every burnt sacrifice was offered with incense, especially the daily lambs every morning and evening. The smoke filled the Holy of Holies through the opening between the veil and the sloping roof.

On the Day of Atonement, the incense altar provided a smoky layer that partially screened God's presence on the mercy seat from the priest's view when he entered the Holy of Holies to sprinkle the sacrificial blood (see Leviticus 16:12). In the Temple of Solomon it was "the whole altar that belonged to the inner sanctuary" (1 Kings 6:22). The psalmist likened his heart to such an altar, where the scented flame of holy longings drifted into the presence of God, as he whispered, "Let my prayer be counted as incense before thee" (Psalm 141:2).

Malachi prophesied the Church's sacrifices and prayers with incense:

> For from the rising of the sun to its setting my name is great among the nations, and in every place incense is offered to my name, and a pure offering; for my name is great among the nations, says the LORD of hosts (Malachi 1:11).

These types are fulfilled in the Church where non-Jews offer incense and prayers with the pure, daily offering of the Eucharistic sacrifice of the Lamb of God, slain but alive on Catholic altars all over the world, just as he is presented to us in the heavenly temple (see Revelation 5:6). The five grains of incense pushed into the Paschal candle at Easter Vigil remember the Five Wounds of Christ our Lamb.

194 | *Fulfilled: Uncovering the Biblical Foundations of Catholicism*

Later Jewish writings also depicted heaven as a place of fragrance. Scripture reveals the incense altar in St. John's view of the heavenly temple where an angel offers incense with prayer (see Revelation 8:3-5). The Tabernacle, the Church, the soul, and the heavenly temple, are all houses of prayer, as it is written, "My house shall be called a house of prayer" (Matthew 21:13).

PRAYER IS THE SOUL BREATHING

"This mystery, then, requires that the faithful believe in it, that they celebrate it, and that they live from it in a vital and personal relationship with the living and true God. This relationship is prayer" (CCC 2558).

Tabernacle incense was a type and symbol of the prayers of the saints. The *Catechism* tells us the psalms are the prayer of the assembly and the masterwork of prayer in the Old Testament. They nourished and expressed the prayer of the people gathered during the great feasts at Jerusalem and each Sabbath in the synagogues. "They extend to all dimensions of history, recalling God's promises already fulfilled and looking for the coming of the Messiah" (CCC 2596).

Jesus also gave us the Lord's Prayer, which St. Augustine believed encapsulates all the prayers of Scripture. Because it is a summary of the gospel, St. Thomas Aquinas considered the Lord's Prayer to be the most perfect of prayers. In the Son, our prayers to the Father are not "vain repetitions," even if they are repetitive. According to the Bible, it is the heart that prays. If our heart is far from God, the words of prayer are in vain. And formalism is an empty censer. Jesus taught that those who pray to be seen have their reward. Non-Catholics accuse Catholics of such vain repetitions, an indictment that would have utterly scandalized the apostles, whose fixed-hour prayer was built on their Jewish practice. But Jesus does not give us a formula to repeat mechanically. Jesus not only gives us the words of our prayer; at the same time he gives us the Spirit by whom these words become in us "spirit and life." Spirit in Scripture is *breath.* So long as the heart is engaged, prayer is the soul breathing.

THE WORD IS GOD BREATHING

Surely no biblical consideration of incense as a type of prayer of the Church could be complete without a mention of *lectio divina,* which is prayer with Scripture itself. All Scripture, Old Testament and New Testament, is "inspired by God" (2 Timothy 3:16). When God created the cosmos in Genesis, the Holy Spirit hovered, breathing over the face of the deep, and there was light and life when "God said" (Genesis 1:3). When the time of fulfillment had come, the Holy Spirit hovered again, and through the breath of his Word, there was a new spiritual light and life (see John 1). "Behold, I make all things new," the Word said from his throne in the heavenly tabernacle, where the incense and prayers of the saints swirl. "Write this, for these words are trustworthy and true" (Revelation 21:5).

As in the Old Testament Tabernacle, where breaths of fragrant incense rose and lingered between the sanctuary and the Holy of Holies, we exchange breath with God by praying with his Word. God breathes his life-giving Word into us, and we exhale our prayer back to him.

"YES" IS MARY'S BREATH

In an address in St. Peter's Square on May 31, 2013, Pope Francis compared our ability to pray with the Word with that of Our Lady, calling Mary the "mother of listening." In his address, Pope Francis followed Mary through her personal practice of prayerful listening to the Word of God, outlining how practically and beautifully she illustrates the traditional steps of *lectio divina:* She prays with the Word; she receives the breath of God in it; she so *LOVEs* the Word of God that it comes alive within her and is born into the world; and she guides us with a sure hand in how to do the same.

First, Mary *listens* to the Word of God.

Listen

Listening is where we "gather the information" the Holy Spirit wants to communicate to us in Scripture, where he speaks. What gave rise to Mary's act of going to visit her relative Elizabeth? A *word of God's* angel. Elizabeth in her old age has also conceived a son (see Luke 1:36). "Mary knew how to listen to God. Be careful: it was not merely 'hearing,' a superficial word, but it was 'listening,' that consists of attention, acceptance and availability to God."[64]

St. Catherine Emmerich reported in her visions that when Mary received the Word of God at the Annunciation, she was alone in silence, praying for the promised Messiah. Mary is attentive and available, and she accepts God's answer to her prayers through her "yes" of cooperation: She receives the breath of God in his Word.

Is prayer with the Word simply hearing or reading the Bible? If I read passage after passage, book after book of the Bible, have I really prayed if I have not discerned God as a person there and adjusted my life to what I have heard?

Mary goes further than simply hearing or reading the Word in a cerebral way that does not penetrate or move her. In a type of exchange of breaths, she applies it to her circumstances and behavior. She makes it fruitful for herself and us by *observing* its meaning.

Observe

Pope Francis continues:

> Mary also listens to the events, that is, she interprets the events of her life, she is attentive to reality itself and does not stop on the surface but goes to the depths to grasp its meaning. Her kinswoman Elizabeth, who is already elderly, is expecting a child: this is the event. But Mary is attentive to the meaning. She can understand it: "with God nothing will be impossible" (Luke 1:37) ... This is also true in our life: listening to God who speaks to us, and listening also to daily reality, paying attention to people, to events, because the Lord is at the door of our life and knocks in many ways, he puts signs on our path; he gives us the ability to see them. Mary is the mother of listening, of attentive listening to God and of equally *attentive listening to the events of life* (emphasis added).[65]

Mary observes the circumstances and relationships of her life through the Word of God she hears. She ponders its meaning in his presence and rises to obey it. Mary's simple, daily routine is ripe with observance, pregnant with life and meaning.

As such, she illustrates perfectly for us how to live the fragrant "incense" of prayer in the Word.

Am I available to God's Word every morning, or am I distracted through activity, noise, and lack of discipline? Do I read and hear God's Word with a heart that searches for him? Do I obey that Word when I observe its perspective on my life?

Verbalize

When our mother of listening receives the breath of God in her morning prayer, she hugs the secret close. She ponders it in her heart and bears its light and life. The Word is incarnated.

That this glorious miracle has happened draws a stream of praise and poetry and stupendous irony fizzing out of her, as Mary prays the Scripture she has hidden in her heart back to God. Her prayer, modeled on Hannah's from the Old Testament, spreads out in a pool of song that runs up the sides of the hills of history like a wave.

On her way to apply what she has heard and learned, Mary breathes back to God her understanding of his Word. Her excitement, her awe, her humility, her bliss at being included in such a shocking way in his sweeping, saving plan for all of history is preserved forever in the Church's Scripture and Liturgy.

The Word of God that Mary has received and applied erupts from her in the *Magnificat*. This is Mary's Song, the prayer-song of the whole Church.

Entrust

As Mary entrusts her heart and life to God in LOVE, he entrusts his Word to her, and she gives birth to that Word in the world, entrusting him to me and you. "May it be done to me according to your word" (Luke 1:38, NAB). This is the privilege and duty of every soul, but it can only occur if we are praying and abiding in the Word with Mary, the mother of listening.

How much more fruitful and fragrant will my prayer become when I begin truly abiding in Christ's Word on a daily basis? In what matter or relationship is my own formation taking place in which he wants my cooperation? What do the daily readings say about that? How will God use what I learn to spread the fragrance of "incense" to others through me?

LOVE the Word™

LOVE: Listen, Observe, Verbalize, and Entrust. Modeled on the Annunciation, LOVE the Word is *lectio divina* without the Latin, a method of prayer in Scripture that invites our Blessed Mother to guide us in her own personal "listening" practice: L (listen), O (observe), V (verbalize), E (entrust).[66] We learn how to LOVE the Word like Mary, from Mary. She teaches us to interpret the Word we hear and read through the landscape of our lives. She guides us into our own aromatic "yes."

As I breathe with him in Scripture on a daily basis, in the Mass and Lectionary, I can use this helpful acronym to discern his activity and will and *listen,* there, to his voice. I *observe* my relationships and circumstances and how they connect to the Word I receive.

I *verbalize* back to God my thoughts, fears, and feelings about all of it, what response I think he desires from me, what I believe he wants me to do. And I fully *entrust* all that concerns me and its fruitfulness to him.

When I LOVE the Word the way Mary, "mother of listening," teaches me to, I practice praying *with* Christ. My "yes" mingles with his and hers. My prayer bears life and light, and I share the aroma of prayerful LOVE in the world.

In the Catholic Mass, the highest form of Christian prayer, the smoke of incense symbolizes the prayers of the faithful drifting up to join those in heaven and the purification of everything the "incense" of sacrificial prayer touches. Incense creates the ambiance of heaven (seen in Revelation), adding a sense of solemnity and mystery to the Mass. The scent and visual imagery of the smoke remind us of the transcendence of the Mass, which links heaven with earth, and help us to enter into the presence of God. I pray that you will never look at the use of incense in the Mass with the same eyes again.

LET'S REVIEW

This is why the Church uses incense in the Liturgy:

- God commanded the use of incense with the daily sacrifices in the Old Testament Tabernacle and that the practice should remain forever.

- Scripture prophesies that non-Jews will offer a daily, "pure offering" with incense "in every place" (see Malachi 1:11).

- The Catholic Mass is the highest form of prayer and the "source and summit of the Christian life" (CCC 1324),[67] as it is a participation in the heavenly liturgy.

- The Catholic Church combines liturgy, incense, and prayer with the only pure, sacrificial offering possible: that of Jesus' own Body and Blood.

INVITATION

Our Catholic prayer tradition is very rich, rooted in Christ, and backed by the full power of the Church—all the angels and saints and the Church militant all over the world. As the horns on the incense altar indicate, it is sacrificial and very powerful and authoritative. Let us pray.

God Prompt – LOVE the Word ™

 LISTEN: "And he taught, and said to them, 'Is it not written, 'My house shall be called a house of prayer for all the nations'? But you have made it a den of robbers" (Mark 11:17).

 OBSERVE: What robs your prayer time?

When do you find it difficult to pray?

Consider how precious and potent your prayer is when you offer it as a sacrifice in those moments. What comes to mind?

What was the most sacrificial prayer you remember ever praying?

Over and over, Scripture tells us Jesus prayed through the night or went alone to the desert or to the mountain to pray. Where do you pray best?

How is your prayer like incense, "a sweet fragrance" before the Lord?

Do you think about your prayers rising to God as you attend Mass?

VERBALIZE: Lord, I believe that in response to my reading in this chapter, you want me to ...

As I think about my prayer life, I need you to ...

I need more power in prayer here ...

I believe you want me to ...

 ENTRUST: *Take our prayers into the sanctuary of heaven and enable them to make our peace with God. Holy Mary, help the miserable, strengthen the discouraged, comfort the sorrowful, pray for your people, plead for the clergy, intercede for all women consecrated to God. May all who venerate you feel now your help and protection. Be ready to help us when we pray, and bring back to us the answers to our prayers. Amen.*

Holy of Holies

The Veil Is Fulfilled in Flesh

The stunning vintage cross-stitch samplers crafted by my mother's respectful fingers might take your breath away. A lifelong "stitcher" and one-time shop owner, she labors in the joys and frustrations of her hobby as any craftsman or craftswoman does.

Hundreds of thousands of colorful hand-stitches and hours of painstaking concentration and deliberation go into these linens of love, such as this Quaker Sampler called *Vierlande 1826*. Doesn't it make your soul sigh just to look at the joy that left her hand? Delicate finery is fearfully, wonderfully made.

The Old Testament Tabernacle included something similar. Within the sanctuary, or Holy Place, of the Tabernacle, there was an inner room called the Holy of Holies, or the Most Holy Place. Judging from the superlative form of its name, we can see that it was a most sacred room, a place no ordinary person could enter. Sort of a dwelling within the dwelling, this mysterious inner room was God's special inner chamber in the Tabernacle, where he dwelt with his people in the cloud and fire.

The word "veil" in Hebrew means a screen, a divider or separator that hides. Like the Tabernacle itself, the pillar of fire and smoke, Jesus' parables, and almost everything else about God's dealings with us, the veil both invited and hid the way into God's innermost presence. No one was allowed behind this veil. In fact, anyone except the high priest who entered the Holy of Holies would die. Even the high priest, God's chosen, specially consecrated mediator, could only pass through the veil and enter this sacred dwelling once a year, on the Day of Atonement, and only by bringing in sacrificial blood with him. The veil showed the barrier between man and God and emphasized that God cannot be trifled with, as he told Moses, "for man shall not see me and live" (Exodus 33:20). The veil protected the people from the danger of God's undiluted holiness, as a barrier to carelessness and irreverence.

The presence of God remained shielded from man behind a thick curtain of smoke and fire and veil throughout the history of Israel; that is, until Jesus' crucifixion, when the curtain in the Jerusalem Temple was torn in half top to bottom. Only God could have carried out such an incredible feat, because the veil was too high for human hands to have reached, and too thick tear. Woven by the consecrated virgins who lived near the Temple, the veil was a scaled, more permanent replica of the wilderness Tabernacle. It stretched about sixty feet in height, thirty feet in width, and four inches thick, yet it was ripped from the top down during the darkness and earthquake accompanying Jesus' death (see Matthew 27:45-54). In fact, this earthquake and modern analysis of its Dead Sea seismic activity make it possible to pinpoint April 3, AD 33 as the probable day of Jesus' crucifixion.[68]

As the Sacrifice was accepted, the veil was torn, and the Holy of Holies was exposed. God's presence was now accessible to all. Shocking as it must have been to the priests ministering in the Temple that day, it is indeed good news for us, because it is evidence that Jesus' sacrificial blood has atoned for our sins and reconciled us to God.

As Jesus cried out, "It is finished" (John 19:30) on the Cross, he was indeed proclaiming that the age of animal offerings was over now that the ultimate offering had been sacrificed. We can now enter into God's presence, "the inner shrine behind the curtain, where Jesus has gone as a forerunner on our behalf" (Hebrews 6:19-20).

POLES AND THORNS

Much like modern curtains do, this thick curtain hung between the Holy Place and the Holy of Holies from rings and clasps attached to wooden poles, or "pillars," overlaid with gold (see Exodus 26). As was every piece of wood used in the Tabernacle, the poles were made of acacia wood.

Also called the "umbrella thorn" for its flat-topped crown of umbrella-shaped leaves, acacia is similar to our cedar or teak in that it is resistant to rot and to our locust in the thorns covering its branches. The prolific acacia tree's shallow roots can extract any moisture from the soil above the hard pan; it tolerates the extensive summertime heat and drought as well as the dry, salty, and alkaline soils of arid Mediterranean and African climates. The acacia is the familiar classic canopy widely pictured in African savannahs such as the Serengeti.

Notably, biblical manna is believed by some to have been the syrupy honeydew excreted by insects that feed on acacia trees. In warm, dry climates, the excretion quickly thickens into sugar lumps and is easily collected as it rains down from the heavily-infested trees. The spiny thorns of the acacia are interspersed with small hook thorns in the same shape as the horns at the corners of the altars of sacrifice and incense, a significance no ancient Hebrew would have ever missed. Somehow these acacia thorns seem to speak of authority and suffering.

Natives call the acacia a "hook and prick" tree for its thorns, and one can only imagine the difficulty and pain involved in stripping away the leaves and thorns in order to prepare the wood for use. Perhaps this is why the word "acacia" means "to pierce" or "to scourge." The veil, then, which was the only way into the inner chamber of the Holy of Holies and foreshadowed the flesh of Christ, hung suspended from poles named for the word for "pierce" or "scourge." *And* that same torture pole is a "manna" tree.

OBEDIENCE IS BETTER THAN SACRIFICE

Can you see, now, why God was so protective of the minutiae regarding how sacred things were made, treated, and practiced in the Old Testament, such that presumption or neglect was punishable by death? He was preserving the types that all these tiny details foreshadowed, so that one day, after millennia had gone by, the Promise could come and fulfill every single one. Jesus said:

Think not that I have come to abolish the law and the prophets; I have come not to abolish them but to fulfil them. For truly, I say to you, till heaven and earth pass away, not an iota, not a dot, will pass from the law until all is accomplished. Whoever then relaxes one of the least of these commandments and teaches men so, shall be called least in the kingdom of heaven; but he who does them and teaches them shall be called great in the kingdom of heaven (Matthew 5:17-19).

That means us. We must not grow lax in our attention to our reverence and obedience to his Word. We must preserve the sacredness of our holy spaces: the Mass, the Eucharist, our homes, our bodies, and our lives. Not out of fear or duty, but for love of his careful forethought, his supreme intelligence, and his mercy, honor, and glory. We must share all of these types and fulfillments that are part of our Catholic heritage with others. In doing so, we grow "great" in the kingdom of Christ.

If the Israelites had loved him less, if they had neglected careful obedience, or if Jesus had neglected obedience in love after them, God's miraculous forethought, astonishing providence, and supernatural preservation in every specific could never be known. Be sure that his command is never arbitrary; his punishments are always instructive.

No wonder Jesus said, "I am the gate" (John 10:9, NAB), and "I am the way" (John 14:6); no wonder the veil in the Temple was torn in two as his body was "pierced for our sins" (Isaiah 53:5, NAB), when Jesus died with his last prayerful exhalation on that scourging pole and opened the way for us into the heavenly holy of holies:

Therefore, brethren, since we have confidence to enter the sanctuary by the blood of Jesus, by the new and living way which he opened for us through the curtain, that is, through his flesh ... let us draw near with a true heart in full assurance of faith (Hebrews 10:19-22).

When the high priest entered the Holy of Holies in the Old Testament Tabernacle on the Day of Atonement, he made meticulous preparations: he washed, robed in special clothing, carried burning incense in with him so the smoke covered his eyes from a direct view of God, and brought in blood to make atonement for sins. Jesus is the fulfillment of all these in the New Testament.

Jesus, our High Priest and Victim, has entered behind the veil and offered his blood sprinkled on the mercy seat (see 1 John 2:2). Jesus *is* our mercy seat, the place where God's justice and mercy kiss (see Psalm 85:10).

> For Christ has entered, not into a sanctuary made with hands, a copy of the true one, but into heaven itself, now to appear in the presence of God on our behalf. Nor was it to offer himself repeatedly, as the high priest enters the Holy Place yearly with blood not his own ... But as it is, he has appeared once for all at the end of the age to put away sin by the sacrifice of himself (Hebrews 9:24-26).

The Holy of Holies was a representation of heaven itself, God's innermost heart and dwelling place, to which we now have access through Christ. "But into the second only the high priest goes, and he but once a year, and not without taking blood which he offers for himself and for the errors of the people" (Hebrews 9:7).

SING WITH THE CHERUBIM

Another important element was the veil's decoration. Made of fine linen twined from blue, purple, and scarlet yarn, images of cherubim were woven into the veil with gold thread. The cherubim also covered the mercy seat inside the Holy of Holies; they were embroidered on the rich, innermost layer of the tent covering, under the coarser, protective goat skins, so that if one looked upward, he would see the cherubim figures "flying" around the sanctuary (see Exodus

26:1, 36) and standing guard before the Holy of Holies. Altogether, the cherubim demonstrated that the Presence is attended and guarded by angelic hosts.

Angels are actively engaged in unceasing praise of God. At Mass, several parts of our Liturgy come from scriptural accounts of angelic worship. The Gloria begins with words sung by the angels at Christ's birth (see Luke 2:14). The *Sanctus* is from Isaiah's vision of God surrounded by angels, who sing, "Holy, holy, holy is the LORD of hosts; the whole earth is full of his glory" (Isaiah 6:3).

Some angels are called cherubim, thought to be from the root "to mount." The psalms describe a majestic God "mounted" upon, or riding, the exotic winged cherubim: "He rode on a cherub, and he flew; and he came swiftly upon the wings of the wind" (Psalm 18:10).

This sort of ascendance imagery is also used in the fifteen songs that comprise one of the most precious and beautiful portions of the Bible, the Psalms of Ascent. Sung by the children of Israel as they ascended Mount Zion in Jerusalem during liturgical feasts, their worship was an integral part of the sweaty, joyful exertion and anticipation of arriving at the summit where God awaited.

Their physical climb up the mountain was a type, model, and picture of the slow upward trajectory of the Christian spiritual life here on earth. It is a glorious enterprise that will ultimately require our very last breath, but those same Psalms of Ascent lift and accompany us, too, up the grand, grueling mountain as we sing them in the Divine Office and our hearts ascend to God in daily prayer.

Far from baby-faced, Ezekiel's vision of the mysterious cherubim reveals a strange, soaring figure, understood to signify a four-part natural possession of the "the intelligent wisdom of man, the lithe strength of the lion, the ponderous weight of the ox, the soaring sublimity of the eagle."[69] This enigmatic hybrid creature, then, symbolizes the cosmos upon which God mounts and presides, enthroned.

Remember that the Tabernacle was considered a mini-cosmos and the Holy of Holies its Garden of Eden. Cherubim are first mentioned in Genesis 3:24, where God placed them at the eastern end, the entrance, of the Garden of Eden to "guard the way to the tree of life." Later, the entrance curtains to the Tabernacle and the Temple, modeled on the Garden, were decorated with these beautiful weavings, artistic renderings of cherubim in vibrant colors and fabrics. At God's instruction, cherubim were depicted on both the Tabernacle and Temple veils that screened the Holy of Holies where God's presence rested.

Two golden statues of cherubim stood at either side of the mercy seat on top of the Ark of the Covenant. Their mysterious wings covered their faces and spread completely over the Ark, functioning somewhat as armrests on the "throne" of the invisible God of Israel. That God's presence was "located" above the Ark of the Covenant, over and between the cherubim, also suggests that the cherubim were "mounts" upon which he "ascended" and "ruled."

God's instructions for the craftsmanship of the cherubim over the Ark's mercy seat were specific. There would be two cherubim on the mercy seat, both of one slab of hammered, beaten gold like the menorah (lampstand). "The cherubim shall spread out their wings above, overshadowing the mercy seat with their wings, their faces one to another; toward the mercy seat shall the faces of the cherubim be" (Exodus 25:20). For us earth dwellers, these elevated scriptural depictions tell us a bittersweet secret about worship.

O GOD BEYOND ALL PRAISING

God dwells amid the praise of cherubim and of men. Indeed, he draws near to it, so that he would be one with it, mount it like the wings of angels, and rule the heaving cosmos from it. He is seated, "enthroned on the praises of Israel" (Psalm 22:3). He inhabits it. Like the cherubim, woven into the veil and beaten and hammered from gold in the dark secret of the Holy of Holies, we must sing!

When circumstances have reduced your joy to a whisper, you must *sing*. When we least feel like it, when it is most difficult, praise is most sacrificial and therefore most potent. Raise your voice in golden praise. Chant the glorious Psalms of Ascent that lift battered spirits to the divine summit.

Cry if you must, if through weakness, anguish, struggle, or discouragement, but it is when life has pierced you through, and hammered and beaten you down, that you are nearest the seat of the mercy of God. He is near to the brokenhearted (see Psalm 34:18). But perhaps the most glorious thing about the veil is why it was "twined," or woven (see Exodus 26:31-34).

ANATOMY, A WOVEN VEIL

The word used in the Old Testament to describe the woven veil hiding the presence of God from human eyes in the Holy of Holies is *sakak* in Hebrew, meaning "covered." Sometimes it describes the worshiping cherubim on the Ark whose wings "covered" the mercy seat. Frequently, it refers to the Temple veil: "And he [Moses] brought the ark into the tabernacle, and set up the veil of the screen, and screened [covered] the ark of the testimony; as the LORD had commanded Moses" (Exodus 40:21, emphasis added). The word *sakak* is used almost exclusively in the Bible to describe the veiling of the presence of God in the Old Testament Tabernacle. With a notable exception.

Psalm 139:15 rejoices, "My frame was not hidden from thee, when I was being made in secret." Earlier in the chapter, verse 13 marvels, "Thou didst form my inward parts, thou didst knit me together in my mother's womb." The word "knit" is *sakak,* also sometimes translated "wove" or "woven" to be a "covering." David sings that his being was woven together secretly by God. Often this section of the Bible is used by pro-life activists to emphasize the inherent sacredness of conception and birth, the invisible invasion of created body by God-breathed soul in the protected covering of a mother's person.

But even more sacred is that the psalmist used this word to describe his own flesh, stating in the most delicate poetry that his body, your body, was prepared to veil the presence of God—that one day each person's anatomy should become the Tabernacle of God: "Do you not know that your body is the temple of the Holy Spirit within you, which you have from God?" (1 Corinthians 6:19). God personally designed and knit every soul and body with the express intention that it should become a home for God himself.

The Old Testament Tabernacle veil teaches that you are also uniquely "stitched" together with a similar unrepeatable purpose, careful respect, and wondrous appreciation. Do not doubt your wonderful nature, for you are "fearfully and wonderfully made" (Psalm 139:14).

FEARFULLY AND WONDERFULLY MADE

Do not doubt your wonderful nature. The King James Version of the Bible that I grew up with reads, "You have covered me in my mother's womb. I will praise thee; for I am fearfully and wonderfully made" (Psalm 139:13). (The RSV-CE translation of this passage includes verse 14 and is slightly different: "Thou art fearful and wonderful. Wonderful are thy works.") In this translation, the word "covered" is *sakak,* the word we mentioned earlier that is used in the Bible almost exclusively to describe the veil.

Here, the word "fearfully" means "reverently," "respectfully." I am formed with reverence and respect.

What a tender thought.

What does it mean to make something respectfully? God is an artist, the ultimate artist. When my mother stitches those vintage samplers, she does not just grab random threads and linens and begin arbitrarily sewing. If an artist creates something respectfully, she takes the time to plan, she thinks through each stitch and step, and she counts carefully. She has chosen a particular pattern and knows what it will look like before she even starts sewing.

An artist might devise a specific statement or emotion to convey with his artistry. He may plant subtle messages that make people think about society, or a bold meaning calling viewers to change, or he may create a work simply to evoke happiness in those that experience it. But it is all planned. Once the work is completed, it will not be discarded or thrown away; it communicates something about its creator; the artist has left part of himself there. It will be intended to hang or rest in a certain location to accomplish a purpose. More so than any human artist, God never clones a work; it is unrepeatable. Just like a masterpiece, God makes each person with a specific plan to accomplish certain things and convey certain messages, says John Henry Newman:

> God has created me to do him some definite service. He has committed some work to me which he has not committed to another. I have my mission—I never may know it in this life, but I shall be told it in the next ... I am a link in a chain, a bond of [connection] between persons. He has not created me for naught. I shall do good, I shall do

his work; I shall be an angel of peace, a preacher of truth in my own place, while not intending it, if I do but keep his commandments and serve in my calling. Therefore, I will trust him. Whatever, wherever I am, I can never be thrown away. If I am in sickness, my sickness may serve him, in perplexity, my perplexity may serve him; if I am in sorrow, my sorrow may serve him ... He does nothing in vain ... He knows what he is about. He may take away my friends, he may throw me among strangers, he may make me feel desolate, make my spirits sink, hide my future from me—still he knows what he is about.[70]

Just visit a zoo. One thing that strikes you about creation is its diversity. God loves differentness. Even among a field of daisies, there are differences in height, leaf structure, vibrancy of petal and stamen color, location, and neighboring weeds.

The saints are distinct. Even if they are similar in temperament or personality or historical setting, there is no single pattern of holiness, no one way of following Christ. There is Moses who flew into a rage and broke the Ten Commandments into pieces, and Gideon who was so timid he repeatedly asked God if he was sure. Joseph the grain-counter accountant, and David the dancing poet-warrior. Paul, the towering intellectual, and Peter the fisherman.

St. Teresa of Calcutta bathed lepers, and Martin Luther King Jr. marched in the streets. Dorothy Day fed the homeless in the city, and St. Maximillian Kolbe starved in a concentration camp. Louis IX lived in luxury, and St. Francis of Assisi chose poverty. St. Judith drove a spike into the enemy's brain, and St. Thérèse of Lisieux leaves roses everywhere she goes.

Each of these was dissimilar, but all are one in Christ. Each found sanctity by reflecting some aspect of the divine reality in simply being who and what he or she was made so reverently and respectfully to be. We cannot imitate any of them exactly, or else we do a disservice to the reverence and respect with which *we* were made and the purpose we are meant to fulfill.

No one can follow God's plan for my life, because no one else has the same strengths, weaknesses, interests, abilities, quirks, or opportunities that are unique to me. I am called to give myself away in love in ways that you are not. And the thing is, I am unable to do that at all if I do not embrace who I am.

Of course, I will wander from my true nature, sometimes in ignorance, sometimes on purpose; that's called sin, which opposes God and ourselves. But not even sin can prevent me from fulfilling the reverence and respect for which I was meant: not Adam's sin, not personal sin, and not the eternal consequences of sin. All that's left is to wrestle with suffering, illness, death, frailty, and the tendency to sin, but none of that can harm those who do not consent to temptation to sin or despair but resist through the graces of Christ (see CCC 1263–1264). God defines me. My fearful and wonderful nature defines me.

I must not try to imitate any one saint exactly. I can look to them all, study their unique holiness, but then I must allow that specific reverence God wants to express through me to come forward. I am respectfully and wonderfully made, woven together like the Tabernacle curtain at the entrance to the Holy of Holies. By simply being wholly and fully myself, minus sin, I am a veil that shelters yet announces the presence of Christ.

LET'S REVIEW

This is why the Church guards the sanctity of life from cradle to grave:

- The most sacred place on the face of the earth in the Old Testament was the Holy of Holies, the innermost chamber of the Tabernacle.

- The Holy of Holies was shrouded by a veil to protect the mysterious secrecy and sacredness where God's presence dwelt.

- The Tabernacle veil was used to wrap the Ark of the Covenant for protection when the Israelites journeyed through the wilderness.

- The words used in describing the delicate weaving of the veil are used to describe how God weaves the flesh as a screen for the human soul.

- Jesus said his body is a temple.

- Scripture says my body is a temple.

- The body is a veil for the "holy of holies" of the soul.

- The Catholic Church is the only Christian church that still follows apostolic teaching on life issues from cradle to grave.

INVITATION

In his encyclical letter *Redemptor Hominis,* John Paul II taught about the dignity that God invested in human flesh. Through his redemption in Christ, man becomes a new creature:

> In this dimension man finds again the greatness, dignity and value that belong to his humanity. In the mystery of the Redemption man becomes newly "expressed" and, in a way, is newly created.[71]

The Catechism of the Catholic Church also teaches this, as explained by Carl Olson, a contemporary Catholic writer:

> By entering into human history and uniting himself with mankind, God not only restored communion between the divine and the natural, he modeled divine sonship for us. By becoming united to humanity, he demonstrated that man can become one with God. Man can become by grace what the Son is by nature. Put another way, the Son of God became a Son of Man so that men might become sons of God (see CCC 460).[72]

Let us pray.

God Prompt – LOVE the Word™

 LISTEN: "Do you not know that your body is the temple of the Holy Spirit within you, which you have from God? You are not your own; you were bought with a price. So glorify God in your body" (1 Corinthians 6:19-20).

 OBSERVE: Remembering that the Tabernacle veil was beautifully embroidered with cherubim, what is God saying to you about your own body?

Human anatomy screens the presence of God in the soul from ordinary eyes. Does this fact make you see others you meet in the marketplace differently?

St. Teresa of Calcutta spoke repeatedly about Jesus in "distressing disguise." While she spoke specifically of the poor, it is also true of other things. Who in your life is currently most distressing to you?

How could this person be Jesus in disguise?

 VERBALIZE: Lord, the most meaningful statement or passage of Scripture through which you spoke to me in this chapter was ...

Lord, I believe that in response to my reading in this chapter, you want me to ...

I need your help to see you in this distressing disguise ...

When I think about people that I dislike, and that you are hidden in them, I feel you saying you want me to ...

 ENTRUST: *"O LORD, thou hast searched me and known me. Thou knowest when I sit down and when I rise up; thou discernest my thoughts from afar. Thou searchest out my path and my lying down, and art acquainted with all my ways. Even before a word is on my tongue, lo, O LORD, thou know it altogether ... For thou didst form my inward parts, thou didst knit me together in my mother's womb. I praise thee, for thou art fearful and wonderful. Wonderful are thy works!" (Psalm 139:1-4, 13-14).*

The Throne of God

The Ark Is Fulfilled in Mary

*A*fter being unable to do so for years due to my speaking schedule, I am teaching RCIA again at my parish. I sorely missed it and felt my teaching juices really come alive that first week back. I began that class the way I always had: with a warning.

In my experience as a religious education director and RCIA facilitator, I have found that people come into the Church for many reasons. Some enter for a future spouse, some are attracted by the "smells and bells," and some wander in seeking the next new thing in their lives. But when someone approaches the Catholic Church in a search for truth, they always seem to encounter a stumbling block with some doctrine or an entire subject they feel unable to agree with, do not believe, and generally have a hard time accepting. I begin each RCIA season with a warning to anticipate this occurrence if it has not already happened, and to try to remain calm in the discomfort until I can thoroughly explore the issue with them to their satisfaction. I do not cajole or attempt to convince; that is the Holy Spirit's job entirely (see John 16:8). I simply stand ready to welcome them home and pray they can yield enough to step past the welcome mat.

For me, that stumbling block issue was Mary. Not until I discovered how the Church Fathers understood her to be the ark of the New Covenant and great sign of the Church, did I truly receive Mary as my own.

HOLY OTHER

Behind the veil in the Holy Place rested the Ark of the Covenant. The Ark was a small box, literally, a "coffin," made of acacia wood and covered with gold, which clearly speaks of particular suffering that was somehow especially divine, divinity somehow "overlaying" humanity. The Ark was the only item in the dark, silent, secret Holy of Holies where the presence of God churned in the pillar of cloud and fire. The stipulations were clear that, because of its supreme holiness, no man was to directly touch the Ark.

Typically, when we think of holiness, we think cleanliness or purity. The word "holy" literally means "other," "set apart," "sanctified," and "consecrated." In the Old Testament, things and people were *set apart* exclusively for God, for the worship of God, or for God himself to work, speak, and rule through. To preserve this unique *otherness,* sacred things and people were not to be "used" or even touched in ordinary ways.

The ancient Jews used repetition to express the superlative of holiness. For instance, we say holy, holier, holiest; they said, "Holy, holy, holy, is the Lord God Almighty" (Revelation 4:8). To the Jewish mind, this otherness and holiness means more along the lines of *transparency.* God is holy because he is who he is and nothing else. He says of himself, "For I the LORD do not change" (Malachi 3:6). Elsewhere, it says that in him, "there is no variation or shadow due to change" (James 1:17).

In the Bible, glimpsing this transparency, this otherness, is felt as fear. The people trembled, for instance, at the base of Mount Sinai when God "descended" at its summit, at the terror and danger of God "appearing" to them in the theophany at the revelation of his Law. Isaiah exclaimed, "Woe is me!" at his vision of God in the heavenly temple. Even after living with Jesus for years, when St. John saw a vision of him reigning in the heavenly temple, he "fell at his feet as though dead." Why is God's holiness so dangerous and terrifying? Because, as John Henry Newman put it so exquisitely, in God's absolute clarity, he *sees* who we *are,* and in him who is utterly transparent, we see ourselves as we really are too:

> Each of us must come to the evening of life. Each of us must enter on eternity. Each of us must come to that quiet, awful time, when we appear before the Lord of the Vineyard, and answer for the deeds done in the body, whether they be good or bad. That, my dear brethren, you will have to undergo ... It will be the dread moment of expectation, when your fate for eternity is in the balance, and when you are about to be sent forth the companion of saints or devils without possibility of change. There can be no change, there can be no reversal. As that judgment decides it, so it will be for ever and ever. Such is the particular judgment ... [when we] find ourselves by ourselves, one by one, in his presence, and ... have brought before us most vividly all the thoughts, words and deeds of this past life. Who will be able to bear the sight of himself? And yet we shall be obliged steadily to confront ourselves and to see ourselves. In this life we shrink from knowing our real selves. We do not like to know how sinful we are. We love those who prophesy smooth things to us, and we are angry with those who tell us of our faults. But then, not one fault only, but all the secret, as well as evident, defects of our

character will be clearly brought out. We shall see what we feared to see here, and much more. And then, when the full sight of ourselves comes to us, who will not wish that he had known more of himself here, rather than leaving it for the inevitable day to reveal it all to him![73]

The more different from God we are, and the further our will is from his, the less pure our love is, and the more terrifying he seems to us. Part of the Old Testament way God communicated his holy otherness was through increasing degrees of consecration that included each of the ones before, such as the Levite hierarchy. The people were consecrated by their adherence to the Law; the Levites were held to that standard and consecrated more by specific disciplines and privileges; Aaron's sons were increasingly so; the stipulations for the high priest included all those prior and were even more stringent due to his responsibilities and duty to make atonement for the entire people by entering the Holy of Holies itself with sacrificial blood.

The more consecrated a thing is, the stronger God's grace and presence is in it and through it. The closer a Tabernacle implement was to the Holy of Holies, the holier and more set apart it was, and the more dangerous its proximity to God's undiluted presence. The Ark was the most secret item in the Tabernacle, completely separated from every human being by the veil and the Presence on it, except for the single moment of the sprinkling of the blood on the Day of Atonement. It was so dangerous, remember, that the people are said to have tied a rope around the high priest's ankle and listened for the tinkling of the bells on the fringe of his robe while he performed the brief, sacred ceremony.

The poles and rings on the Ark, then, allowed it to be transported safely by the Kohathites without being touched. When in movement, the Ark was wrapped and concealed within the veil of the sanctuary. The Kohathites formed one of the three divisions of the tribe of

Levi, whose quarters in the wilderness were on the southern side of the Tabernacle. Later, in King David's day, the Kohathites became the music ministers. Due to the strict regulations regarding how the sacred implements could be carried, they had special charge of carrying the Ark and the veil and the other sanctuary furnishings (see Numbers 3:29-31).

As the sign of God's unique presence with them, the Ark traveled everywhere with the Israelites, even into battle. To correct a presumptuous superstition into which the people had lapsed regarding the Ark, God allowed it to be taken in a battle with their arch-enemies, the Philistines, under King Saul, and the Israelites were appalled by the rout they suffered. Once King David rose to the throne and subdued the Philistines, he prepared to bring the sacred Ark back to Jerusalem where it belonged. By then, it seems, familiarity lent a sense of nonchalance to the Israelites' treatment of the Ark, which resulted in another shocking tragedy.

DAVID'S MISTAKE

The Philistines had carried the Ark away by cow cart, and King David prepared to bring it back by the same method. But the Law was specific that the Ark was to be carried personally, on the shoulders of the sons of Kohath (see Exodus 25:22), not by cart or any other vehicle. As they praised God with all their might on the way up to Jerusalem, the oxen stumbled, and the Ark became unstable. One of the attendants put out his hand to steady it, and "he died there beside the ark of God" (2 Samuel 6:7). After a flash of anger at God for the sudden deadly force, David's reverence and respect was restored. He marveled, ""How can the ark of the LORD come to me?" (2 Samuel 6:9) in a prophetic utterance that Elizabeth would echo of the new ark centuries later, "And why is this granted me, that the mother of my Lord should come to me?" (Luke 1:43). Thereafter, David was careful to observe legal protocol in moving the Ark.

Its Old Testament history and biblical treatment illustrate God's will that the Ark—where his presence visually manifested—remain untouched and untouchable. Later, because St. Luke's deliberate parallelism is obvious throughout, the Church Fathers understood him to have used 2 Samuel 6 to depict Mary as the new ark in the first chapter of his Gospel (Luke 1:39-56).

Called the "Ark of the New Covenant" by the Church Fathers, Our Lady was intimated by the characteristics of the Ark of the Testimony in the Tabernacle. Located secretly in the Holy of Holies, the inner chamber of the Tabernacle, no man could touch the Ark upon penalty of death. Even the high priest was completely restricted from its vicinity except on the annual Day of Atonement.

It was Mary's purity, then, upon which the presence of the Lord would one day uniquely rest, just as he had once rested on the untouchable Ark, and it was she who would be anointed first with the sacrificial blood of her only son, the Lamb slain from the foundation of the world.

The Ark was secluded on one side by the veil, richly woven in blue, scarlet, and purple thread and embroidered with ornate worshiping cherubim. On the remaining sides, the Ark was protected within the Holy of Holies by wood paneling overlaid with gold. Within this beautiful cocoon, the Ark-coffin, uniquely dedicated to suffering, rested secretly in the most Holy Place of the Tabernacle and bore the presence of God.

In addition, the Ark's lid was decorated with two of the glorious, worshiping cherubim beaten from a single piece of gold, the one piece signifying unity, and the hammered gold signifying sacrificial worship. The cherubim, then, worshiping in perpetual service to

228 | *Fulfilled: Uncovering the Biblical Foundations of Catholicism*

God, enclosed the Ark within the covering of their wings, depicting their role in assisting and surrounding the Ark and secluding it in the privacy and mystery of the sacrificial love of the Trinity.

Inside the small box was the Covenant of the Jewish people signified by the "Ten Words" (the Ten Commandments), a pot of manna, and Aaron's fruited almond rod, just as Mary carried their incarnate fulfilment in her womb.

THE BATTLE OF JERICHO

Carried on the priests' shoulders, the Ark led the people through the wilderness for forty years, all the way to the Jordan River separating the Israelites from the Promised Land. Bearing the Ark's leadership and the cloud of God, it was not until the priests' bare toes touched the waters of faith that the Jordan River separated, in the same way they had at the Red Sea, to allow them to walk through the river on a dry bed. And so they processed across the Jordan into the Promised Land.

This Promised Land would be no picnic, however, for the first thing the people encountered was Jericho, a fortified stronghold whose inhabitants the Israelites had to rout in order to begin making the land their own. By perhaps the most unorthodox method in the history of human warfare, the Israelites brought a coffin-throne (the Ark) to a siege as a weapon (see Joshua 6).

At the command of God, seven trumpet-blowing priests led the people and the Ark in a procession around the city for seven days; trumpets are a scriptural symbol of the voice and Word of God. On the seventh day, after encircling Jericho seven times and ending the procession with shouting and trumpet blowing, the walls of the city fell, and the Israelites took it completely.

The creative, speaking, brooding Holy Spirit "moving" on the face of the Genesis waters (see Genesis 1:2) is the same Spirit, or breath, that rested on the mercy seat of the Ark, filling the Tabernacle, and giving life to the Israelites through what he spoke to Moses (see Exodus 40:34-35); and the same Spirit that "overshadowed" the Virgin Mary, conceiving the Incarnate Word in her womb (see Luke 1:35). In the Septuagint, the exact same word is used in each instance.

For this reason, and several other striking parallels, the early Church Fathers regarded Mary as the ark of the New Covenant. The Ark, on which the Spirit uniquely rested and which accompanied the Israelites on all their journeys, was arguably the most integral part of the battles necessary to take the Promised Land. As Catholics, we can take comfort in having recourse to Mary, our new ark, and can implore her help with prayers like the Memorare:

> Remember, O most gracious Virgin Mary, that never was it known that anyone who fled to thy protection, implored thy help, or sought thy intercession was left unaided. Inspired by this confidence, I fly unto thee, O Virgin of virgins, my Mother; to thee do I come, before thee I stand, sinful and sorrowful. O Mother of the Word Incarnate, despise not my petitions, but in thy mercy, hear and answer me.

THE ARK IN THE HEAVENLY TEMPLE

The book of Second Maccabees records that the prophet Jeremiah hid the original Ark in a cave to preserve it from the Babylonians' destruction of Jerusalem. Josephus wrote of a tradition that remains today among modern Samaritans,[74] that the Ark was hidden on Mount Nebo. But Jeremiah's followers neglected to mark the cave, and its location was lost, so Jeremiah prophesied that it was God's will that it should remain hidden until he revealed its location at the proper time (see 2 Maccabees 2:1-8).

Written right after the destruction of Jerusalem in 586 BC, Lamentations 2:1 says that during the fall of Jerusalem, "He has not remembered his footstool in the day of his anger." Psalm 132:7-8 also speaks of the footstool as the Ark, "'Let us go to his dwelling place; let us worship at his footstool!' Arise, O LORD, and go to thy resting place, thou and the ark of thy might." This Psalm is applied to Mary in the Liturgy, illustrating how the Church regards her as the ark, assumed into God's presence.

The Ark of the Covenant was subsequently lost, captured, or destroyed along with the destruction of Jerusalem in 586 BC, and history testifies that there was no Ark in the Temple after the exile. Jeremiah prophesied such:

> And when you have multiplied and increased in the land, in those days, says the LORD, they shall no more say, 'The ark of the covenant of the LORD.' It shall not come to mind, or be remembered, or missed; it shall not be made again. At that time Jerusalem shall be called the throne of the LORD, and all nations shall gather to it, to the presence of the LORD in Jerusalem (Jeremiah 3:16-17).

They would remember the Ark no more, because it would be fulfilled in an untouchable, virgin Mother of God.

Lost for generations, St. John sees the Ark in in its fulfillment in the heavenly temple (see Revelation 11:19–12:1)—accompanied by thunder, lightning, hail, and earthquake, the traditional signs of theophany—and there is the woman who brought forth the Child who would rule over the nations. She is crowned as queen. According to Church history, she is Mary, the pure and holy ark of the New Covenant:

> Mary, in whom the Lord himself has just made his dwelling, is the daughter of Zion in person, the ark of the covenant, the place where the glory of the Lord dwells. She is "the dwelling of God ... with men"[75] (CCC 2676).

THE UNASSAILABLE APOSTOLIC WITNESS

Because apocalyptic and prophetic literature has more than one fulfillment in the Bible, the Woman of Revelation 12 is symbolic of Israel first, Mary second, and finally, the Church. Non-Catholics maintain the Israel and church interpretations, while disputing that the woman is Mary herself. Aside from the intellectual gymnastics necessary to take such a position (Occam's Razor[76] after all), to deny that this passage refers to Mary is to deny all of Church history itself. The most obvious biblical "woman" who gave birth to a male Child is Mary.

St. Hippolytus (c. 170–c. 236) wrote:

> At that time, the Savior coming from the Virgin, the Ark, brought forth his own Body into the world from that Ark, which was gilded with pure gold within by the Word, and without by the Holy Ghost; so that the truth was shown forth, and the Ark was manifested ... And the Savior came into the world bearing the incorruptible Ark, that is to say his own body. [77]

St. Ephrem (c. 306–373)[78], St. Cyril (315–387)[79], St. Ambrose (c. 339–397)[80], and St. Athanasius (c. 296–373)[81] all call Mary the new ark. Church history is in complete agreement that Mary is the ark of the New Covenant until after the Protestant rebellion.

Marian teachings are not new; they are as old as the Church itself. Throughout history, Church councils always formalized specific teachings when they were challenged by heresies. They formalized Marian doctrines at the Council of Ephesus in AD 431 because there were challenges to Jesus' divinity and humanity. All Marian beliefs flow from the truths of who Jesus is, as "each tree is known by its fruit" (Luke 6:44). What is true of her is true because of her Son. "To separate Christ from his Mother in our piety is to divide Christ

... Where the Mother is left out, the Son is no longer understood," said Blessed Columba Marmion.[82] In retaining the historical understanding of Mary, the Catholic Church demonstrates its Magisterium to be the heir and successor of Saints Luke and John, all of the apostles and their successors, and the early Church.

On the study and interpretation of Scripture, Pope Leo XIII taught:

> The Holy Fathers, we say, are of supreme authority, whenever they all interpret in one and the same manner any text of the Bible, as pertaining to the doctrine of faith or morals; for their unanimity clearly evinces that such interpretation has come down from the Apostles as a matter of Catholic faith.[83]

Blessed John Henry Newman explains, "We receive those doctrines which they thus teach, not merely because they teach them, but because they bear witness that all Christians everywhere then held them."[84]

As a non-Catholic, I read the primary sources when researching my way through Catholic teachings. I could see the Catholic Church had preserved and maintained these teachings from the apostles, but I was having difficulty getting over the stumbling block I faced regarding Mary. For any rational, thinking person, what makes the claims of the Catholic Church regarding Mary as Mother of God so difficult to fathom is the question, "Why?" What possible reason could God have for preserving Mary as both the perpetual ark of the New Covenant and as the sinless, ever-virgin new Eve as Church history and our Christian heritage say he did?

The answer is eschatological and lies in Jesus, all the way forward in salvation history to his second coming and the marriage feast that will consummate the new heavens and new earth. Not until I understood Mary as the great sign of the Church, did her role make sense to me.

THE SIGN OF THE CHURCH

I was thinking too small. My sight was so short. Like Israel's expectation for the Messiah, I journeyed with the Magi to Mary and the baby Jesus in the manger and stopped my Christmas consideration with her human maternity. Every Israelite alive expected a merely human messiah with a regular human kingdom, and every married woman in Israel hoped to be his mother in the normal way. How else could it be?

But only one was "blessed among women," and she through consecrated celibacy. She is "full of grace"—sinless—by a special work of her Savior (see Luke 1:28, 47). She is overshadowed like the first Ark (see Exodus 40:35; Luke 1:35). She is betrothed, but resolved to remain virgin: "How can this be?" (Luke 1:34).

This ever-virgin woman is the fulfillment of Genesis and "portent" of Revelation 12. She is the untouched and untouchable ark, Mother by direct action from God himself with no human intervention, an unimagined, unforeseen possibility up to this point in Israelite and human history. Her new, divine motherhood embraces all of those "who keep the commandments of God and bear testimony to Jesus," her son (Revelation 12:17).

From the moment of his miraculous incarnation within her, God began directing expectations of the messianic kingdom to a "new Israel" and its ultimate spiritual finality: a new Eve for his new Adam, a new ark for his New Covenant, a spotless bride for his Bridegroom.

Jesus affirmed this eschatological long view by directing our own expectations further ahead than human motherhood. His teachings on the absolute indissolubility of marriage and the even higher state of celibacy that he himself chose along with his mother point far beyond themselves. After his resurrection, Jesus held himself apart from those who would cling to his physical manifestations,

234 | *Fulfilled: Uncovering the Biblical Foundations of Catholicism*

disappearing once he was recognized so the Church could begin looking *forward* for him in the Eucharist and the Second Coming (see John 20:17; Luke 24:13-53).

Together, the new Adam and new Eve; the new ark and the New Covenant; the Bridegroom and bride—pure and virgin, celibate but fecund—give spiritual birth to a spiritual kingdom of spiritual children through the Holy Spirit. This kingdom will, for its perfection and divine genesis, endure for all eternity. "He who is able to receive this, let him receive it" (Matthew 19:12).

We are the body of Christ, and Christ was born of Mary. Precisely because the kingdom to come is to be fulfilled in flesh and blood, its beginning is in the Mother. Mary's motherhood is the sign of our New Covenant with God who is himself pure spirit. Her perpetually sinless, virgin motherhood is the beginning and prototype of the Church fulfilled, the spotless bride of Christ. Mary is the great "sign" of the Church as spiritual mother.

She remains both sinless and virgin, because her motherhood is completely, utterly, eternally miraculous and pure—giving birth to the Word in innumerable spiritual children, all conceived by the Holy Spirit and born of God. She nurtures our holiness so that we, too, can give birth to the Word in the world as well through faith.

> Unless one looks to the Mother of God, it is impossible to understand the mystery of the Church, her reality, her essential vitality ... There is an analogy in God's salvific economy: if we wish to understand it fully in relation to the whole of human history, we cannot omit, in the perspective of our faith, the mystery of "woman": virgin-mother-spouse.[85]

LET'S REVIEW

The Catholic Church venerates Mary as the ark of the New Covenant and great sign of the Church because:

- The Ark of the Covenant in the Tabernacle was the place where God's presence dwelt.

- Inside the Ark were symbols of the Old Covenant, all meant to be eternal and fulfilled in Christ.

- Jesus is the New Covenant; Mary carried the New Covenant in her womb and is therefore the new ark.

- In the heavenly temple, the ark is a woman, a queen, who gives birth to a male child who is the King (see Revelation 11:19–12:2).

- In addition to Israel or Zion, the Church has always understood the ark in the heavenly temple to be Mary.

- As the ark of the New Covenant, Mary is the great sign and forerunner of the Church.

INVITATION

The Ark in the Tabernacle was the throne from which God ruled. The Old Testament Ark of the Covenant, Mary, Jesus, the Church collectively, and you and I individually all express this idea. Each is a type of ark. The kingdom of God is within you, meaning, your soul was created to be the throne of God, the place where God rules and rests, hidden within the holy of holies of your heart. Let us pray.

God Prompt – LOVE the Word ™

 LISTEN: "There I will meet with you, and from above the mercy seat, from between the two cherubim that are upon the ark of the testimony, I will speak with you" (Exodus 25:22).

 OBSERVE: One of the functions of the Ark was that of an oracle, meaning God spoke to Moses from the cloud positioned over the mercy seat, and he spoke to the high priest through the *Urim* and *Thummim* stones. In the seclusion, silence and privacy of the inner sanctuary of the Tabernacle, God audibly instructed, guided, and related to his people. Do you expect God to speak to you regarding your circumstances and life?

Remember that the Ark contained the Word of God, a memorial pot of manna, and Aaron's living rod. In what ways should your own life reflect the contents of the Ark?

Is Jesus the ruler of your heart and life? When have you allowed Jesus to be the ruler of your heart most fully?

Spend some time prayerfully reviewing your life and any particular areas in which you still want to be more obedient.

 VERBALIZE: Lord, the most meaningful statement or passage of Scripture through which you spoke to me in this chapter was ...

I believe that in response to my reading in this chapter, you want me to ...

The thing that is the hardest about trying to hear you speak directly to me is ...

ENTRUST: *Hail Mary, full of grace, the Lord is with thee. Blessed art thou among women, and blessed is the fruit of thy womb, Jesus. Holy Mary, Mother of God, pray for us sinners, now and at the hour of our death. Amen*

— At Home in the Tabernacle —

hroughout your exploration of the foundations of your living
Catholic Faith in the Old Testament Tabernacle, God has been
calling you to *dwell* with him more intimately. I bet you haven't
considered that you have been busy building up your very own
spiritual tabernacle during your reading. Whether or not you
realized it, the Master Architect has been leading you as you laid one
"stone" after another, so that you can share it all with others. Let's
review his blueprint for life in Christ.

DIVINE STRUCTURE

The Tabernacle was a portable tent-like structure and a surrounding
external courtyard in which God dwelt in the midst of his people.
The whole compound was surrounded by another fence about seven
feet in height, made of hangings held by poles.

The Tabernacle proper was divided into the Holy Place and the Holy
of Holies. The tent was made of acacia wood boards overlaid with
gold and fitted together to form the walls, measuring forty-five by
fifteen feet. On top, four layers of curtains acted as a roof to shield
the Tabernacle from sun and rain: the innermost layer was woven
in fine linen and embroidered with figures of angelic cherubim; the
second layer was made of goat's hair; and the outer layers were
made of tougher animal skins. Like modern tents, the outer skin
curtains were pinned to the ground with loops and clasps.

The strictly prescribed Tabernacle setup informed the Israelites
that they could only draw near to God in the way he offered. There
was no other way. As we have seen, God used the Old Testament
Tabernacle to tell us that we, too, can only draw near to him most
fully through the means he has provided for us in the historical
Church in Jesus Christ.

JESUS IS THE NEW TABERNACLE

All fulfillment begins with Jesus. Jesus said he did not come to cancel the Old Testament but to give us the grace to keep it more perfectly than just in our outward behavior, so that we fulfill the requirements of the Law ourselves in him (see Matthew 5:17-19, 9:16-17). Jesus came to build something gloriously new on the foundation of the old structure. As the new Tabernacle, he imbues the New Covenant with a new spirit. He teaches us their proper orientation and meaning and gives it all saving power. He says the Old Covenant is not canceled, as in tossed out as "wrong" or "bad," even in its minutia. In fact, Jesus offers his gravest warning to anyone would simply relax, much less eradicate, even one detail. He gathers in, upholds, and expands the entire Old Testament, into and beyond himself, through us, his body and Church. In his resurrected person, he brings it forward and fills it with a breath and grace that makes the new structure alive and therefore capable of salvation.

Let's review all the important elements and how they apply to us in the Church as a faith-sharing model. The shape of the Tabernacle layout is the Cross of Christ. The Church imitates this cruciform shape and proportions in its individual churches. Sharing the Catholic Faith is as simple as drawing a line-sketch of the Tabernacle and its facilities and explaining how each one is uniquely fulfilled in the Catholic Church.

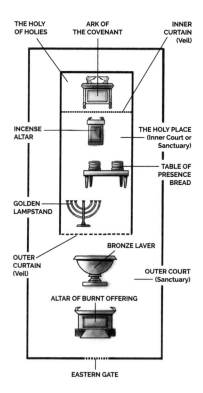

TABERNACLE

First and foremost, the Church is the final, eternal Tabernacle of God as Christ's mystical body. That is an awesome thought, because in the Old Testament, there were times when God withdrew his Spirit from the Tabernacle or Temple because of the people's sins. But after Jesus' perfect sacrifice, that can never happen again. Because the Church is the "house" or tabernacle in the New Testament, as St. Paul says, it is therefore the foundation of truth (see 1 Timothy 3:15).

Because the Church is made of individual Christians, you are also a living tabernacle of God. For God to feel completely at home and dwell most fully in us, every worship element of the Old Testament Tabernacle should be reflected in our own lives. The fullness of the Faith has been preserved in the Catholic Church so that each prescribed element is present in the life of the faithful Catholic today. *The Old Testament Tabernacle is fulfilled in the Catholic Church.*

LITURGICAL YEAR

Observing the liturgical worship schedule of the Church is a happy privilege. Through our liturgical year, we "keep time" with God and all the saints and angels. As in the Old Testament, our special days include rest, offerings, and a sacred assembly.

Holy days and feast days are special because they remind us of important salvation events in our history with God. Jesus fulfilled the Old Testament feasts, so our important holy days revolve around him—Sunday, Christmas, and Easter—and those saints who served him most extravagantly. St. Paul tells us plainly to "celebrate the festival [feast]" (1 Corinthians 5:7-8). Every Catholic holy and feast day is centered on the New Covenant himself, in the Eucharist. *The Old Testament liturgical year is fulfilled in the Catholic liturgical year.*

PRIESTHOOD

As in the Old Testament and Ezekiel's messianic temple, there is both an institutional and lay priesthood in the Catholic Church. "And like living stones be yourselves built into a spiritual house, to be a holy priesthood, to offer spiritual sacrifices acceptable to God through Jesus Christ" (1 Peter 2:5).

Our Catholic priesthood serves God's people through the new sacramental economy founded on Christ in the Eucharist. Every Christian is also called to some form of priesthood. We lay "priests" can offer all our sacrifices in union with Christ for the good of souls. Because Jesus appoints his priests and rules through our Catholic priesthood, obeying Church leadership in their legitimate areas is obeying Christ (see Romans 13:1-2). *The levitical priesthood is fulfilled in the Catholic priesthood.*

THE BRONZE ALTAR

The bronze altar in the Tabernacle was the location for all the bloody, burnt offerings. Jesus is both our High Priest and Victim. He is the ultimate sacrifice, the perfect Lamb of God who takes away the sin of the world. The Cross is his altar and ours, too.

Following in the sacrificial footsteps of Christ, we can offer up our own sufferings as a sacrifice to God for our good and the good of souls. Remember, "Eucharist" means "thanksgiving." We give thanks for Jesus' ultimate sacrifice by taking up the chalice of salvation and calling on the name of the Lord (see Psalm 116:12-13). *The bronze altar is fulfilled in the Catholic sacrificial altar.*

ALTAR FIRE

Throughout the Bible, God revealed his all-consuming love for his people through fire, "For our God *is* a consuming fire" (Hebrews 12:29, emphasis added). What a thrilling thought.

"Set me as a seal upon your heart, as a seal upon your arm; for love is strong as death, jealousy is cruel as the grave. Its flashes are flashes of fire, a most vehement flame" (Songs 8:6). The "fiery trials" and sufferings we experience in our lives are ultimately the presence of God accepting our many offerings throughout the primary offering of our whole life: heart, soul, mind, and strength. This fiery Presence purifies us with the strength of his love, and so he is the fire of purgatory. God, himself, is the fire that purifies and saves us (see 1 Corinthians 3:12-15). *The Tabernacle altar fire is fulfilled in purgatory.*

BRONZE LAVER

All of Christendom agrees that the Old Testament laver foreshadowed the sacrament of baptism. Baptism configures the soul for grace and initiates us into the life of Christ. "Jesus answered, 'Truly, truly, I say to you, unless one is born of water and the Spirit, he cannot enter the kingdom of God'" (John 3:5). Confession keeps the soul clean: "If we confess our sins, he is faithful and just, and will forgive our sins and cleanse us from all unrighteousness" (1 John 1:9). *The Tabernacle laver is fulfilled in confession and baptism.*

THE LAMPSTAND

The lampstand was the only illumination in the holy place of the Old Testament sanctuary. Engraved with beautiful almond branches, flowers, and ripe fruit, it remained in God's presence, symbolizing the almond branch-staff of the high priest. His staff was chosen and confirmed by God as the first high priest and representative of his eternal, institutional priesthood.

The *Urim* and *Thummim* in the high priest's chest pocket also illustrated God's authoritative Word and proper doctrine that came to the people through the priesthood. Jesus is the center of the historical, institutional priesthood of the Church (see Revelation 1:12-13, 20). *The Tabernacle lampstand is fulfilled through the Magisterium of the Church.*

TABLE OF PRESENCE BREAD

The golden Table of Presence Bread in the Tabernacle foreshadowed Jesus, our "super manna." The Catholic Church retains the Old Testament teaching of the real presence of God in the Presence Bread through Christ in the Eucharist.

Our Holy Eucharist is in the presence of God through Christ, but also *is* the eternal Presence of God, tabernacling with us in, with, and through Christ in his Church. The Eucharist is the daily, consistent continuation of God's command that there be perpetual Bread of the Presence in the Tabernacle.

Every time we receive the Eucharist, we draw these ancient truths ever-forward into salvation history. As Psalm 116:17 says, "I will offer to thee the sacrifice of thanksgiving and call on the name of the LORD." Receiving the Eucharist is my offering of *thanksgiving (eucharista)* to God (see Luke 22:19). *The Tabernacle Presence Bread is fulfilled in the Eucharist.*

INCENSE ALTAR

Whenever we pray, especially in the Mass (see Malachi 1:11), and particularly when our prayers are most difficult and sacrificial, our prayer ascends to the heavenly tabernacle before God like incense (see Revelation 5:8-10). He is touched, pleased, and moved by our communal and personal prayers, which are accompanied by those of the angels and saints, who are always offering the "incense" of the Church's prayer to God as a sacrifice. *Tabernacle incense is fulfilled in the Catholic Mass.*

TABERNACLE VEIL

The entrance to the Holy of Holies in the Old Testament Tabernacle was covered by an intricately embroidered tapestry. Woven in vibrant purple, blue, and scarlet threads, and decorated with cherubim, the veil was an artistic rendering of a sacred truth: God's royal, sacrificial presence is covered and guarded by a woven veil and angels—in the Tabernacle, in the flesh of Jesus, and in our own flesh, in varying degrees. Imagine yourself and your neighbor surrounded by angels, and the flesh as the sacred curtain that veils God's presence. *The woven Tabernacle veil is fulfilled in human flesh.*

ARK OF THE COVENANT

The Ark of the Covenant was the "footstool" and throne from which God ruled and spoke in the Tabernacle. The Old Testament Ark of the Covenant foreshadowed Mary and Jesus and then the Church collectively. Ultimately, you and I also individually express this idea; each of us is a type of ark, the place where God rules and rests, hidden within the holy of holies of our hearts. The early Church gave Mary the title of "Ark of the New Covenant" because of the numerous scriptural parallels between her and the Old Testament Ark. We can welcome God's protection and direction and influence in our lives especially by welcoming Mary. *The Tabernacle Ark is fulfilled in Mary.*

UNITY IS A MARK OF THE CHURCH

As I made my way to the Catholic Church, I was overwhelmed by a sense of God's consistency in the Bible and history. I had been taught that the Old Testament was obsolete in the way a sandcastle is obsolete after having been washed away by a wave, or that humanity had destroyed God's plans so completely that he had to erase everything and start anew. But God makes no mistakes, and we cannot destroy his plans.

I went to Mass and saw its similarities with the worship God prescribed in the Old Testament. As my awareness of the Old Testament connections to the Catholic Faith and the Mass grew, I recognized the call home to my full, ancient, saving heritage in the Catholic Church. We have a pope who sits in Peter's chair and bishops and priests ministering to the Lord in true apostolic succession. The Holy Sacrifice of the Mass is offered daily in every season of the year; the prayers of the Church are prayed in every time zone in the world, bathing the whole earth in prayer every hour of every day. Our churches are fragrant with incense and glorious with stained glass and beautiful images; we see crucifixes, lamps, and icons; and our priests are robed in ecclesial vestments. All of this is because we observe the traditions of the ancient Church.

Christ did not wipe out the Old Testament. The Old Testament did exactly what it was designed to do: announce the Savior and prepare the people to recognize and receive him in the Catholic Church. The apostles built and filled Christ's Church on their beautiful, ancient Jewish heritage and foundation.

Jesus' resurrected body illustrates "fulfillment" perfectly: No one would say there was anything "wrong" with Jesus' earthly body; it fulfilled its glorious purpose perfectly, as a vehicle for manifesting and sacrificing God; it was well-worn, poured out, ripped open, and expired; then it was *resurrected* to something greater. It was the same body, but glorified. It was *fulfilled* and offered as Eucharistic nourishment that would raise all of us to eternal life with him. Jesus came in the human bodily state because this was necessary to fulfill and elevate it for us. Jesus' resurrection elevated our fallen humanity to the fullness God always intended for it. All who follow the same path are one with him.

In exactly the same way, the New Covenant was built on the Old Covenant, not as accident or afterthought, but intentionally. The book of Hebrews states numerous times that the New Covenant is "better" (see Hebrews 6:9, 7:19, 8:16, 9:23, 10:34, 11:16, 11:35, 11:40). It is better because it is salvific. The New Covenant embraces the Old Covenant and brings it forward in fabulous, miraculous glory, so that the two are finally one in providential unity.

Jesus prayed, "that they may be one, even as we are one" (John 17:11). Saints Peter and Paul and the martyrs throughout Church history spent their lives in the struggle of that prayer, to bring together into one Church, under one Gospel, those who were divided by differing heritage and belief. I believe *you* can be influential in helping unify Christians by using your faith and knowledge of the Tabernacle to bring someone in your sphere of influence to the Catholic Church. I pray that after reading this book, you better understand our beautiful, ancient Catholic Faith and that you feel confident in sharing it concisely with others using the Old Testament Tabernacle as a convenient faith-sharing model.

My plea is that you understand and communicate how the Old Testament Tabernacle is *the* perfectly packaged biblical model for conveniently understanding and explaining seemingly arbitrary Catholic beliefs and practices that can baffle and frustrate both fallen-away Catholics and non-Catholics.

My longing is that you have mastered the Old Testament Tabernacle as the blueprint and foundation for true faith, and that you appreciate why the Catholic Church must show us all how to practice it, fulfilled as the living tabernacle, the body of Christ on earth. May the Holy Spirit urge you to wade into his scattered people and draw them home to the fulfilment of their faith in his Church. Onward!

LET'S REVIEW

The Catholic Church is the only place the whole-life worship prescribed by God in Scripture is available because:

- God is always calling us to worship in his presence.

- God explains how to worship properly.

- God asks us to make a home for him.

- I am a tabernacle of God.

- Purity in worship makes him feel "at home," and draws me into the closest possible relationship to God.

- Through the Tabernacle, God instructed that proper worship should include certain elements.

- The Old Testament Tabernacle was a copy of the sanctuary in heaven and the prototype of the Church to come.

- The Old Testament Tabernacle was the blueprint and foundation upon which Church worship and practice would be built.

- Jesus fulfills the Old Testament Tabernacle and all its elements.

- God lives in and is present to the world through the Tabernacle of the Church.

- For two-thousand years, Catholic Liturgy and worship, through Jesus—the true and final Tabernacle—has included a liturgical schedule; an institutional priesthood; a real altar; true sacrifice; purifying fire; baptismal waters; magisterial light; Eucharistic Presence Bread; fragrant prayer; guardianship of the veil; and the ark of the New Covenant.

- Through Christ, every type in the Old Testament Tabernacle has been brought forward as true antitype, alive and fully invested with saving grace, *fulfilled* in the Catholic Church.

INVITATION

"Now you are the body of Christ and individually members of it" (1 Corinthians 12:27). Everything that Jesus fulfilled on earth and continues in the heavenly temple is brought forward in time through his body, the Church. In order to dwell in the closest possible relationship to God and truly be the body of Christ on earth, the Church *must* include all of the elements of the Old Testament Tabernacle, the messianic temple prophecies, and the heavenly worship we see in the Bible.

"Christ is the true temple of God, 'the place where his glory dwells'; by the grace of God, Christians also become the temples of the Holy Spirit, living stones out of which the Church is built" (CCC 1197).

The Catholic Church is the only Church on earth that has retained every element. Catholic faith and worship is true, heavenly worship. Let us pray.

God Prompt – LOVE the Word ™

 LISTEN: "Then he said to me, 'Prophesy to the breath, prophesy, son of man, and say to the breath, Thus says the Lord GOD: Come from the four winds, O breath, and breathe upon these slain, that they may live.' So I prophesied as he commanded me, and the breath came into them, and they lived, and stood upon their feet, an exceedingly great host" (Ezekiel 37:9-10).

OBSERVE: How has this book enriched your worship experience at Mass and in personal prayer?

Are you more convinced of the biblical reasons the Catholic Church worships and practices the way it does?

Do you feel more confident in your ability to share the biblical roots of Catholic faith with those you know and love?

How is each of the elements of the Tabernacle active in your own life?

In what area of your life do you need to feel God's presence more strongly?

 VERBALIZE: Lord, after this book, I feel your presence more deeply here ...

But I still have questions about ...

Lord, I need to know that you love me unconditionally, even though the tabernacle of my body and heart is not always pure enough to welcome you ...

Now that I know my Church better, I promise to ...

 ENTRUST: *Hail, Holy Queen, Mother of mercy, our life, our sweetness, and our hope. To thee do we cry, poor banished children of Eve; to thee do we send up our sighs, mourning and weeping in this valley of tears. Turn, then, most gracious advocate, thine eyes of mercy toward us, and after this, our exile, show unto us the blessed fruit of thy womb, Jesus. O clement, O loving, O sweet Virgin Mary. Amen.*

NOTES

1. *Catholic Herald,* "Full text: Cardinal Sarah at Sacra Liturgia conference," July 12, 2016, accessed December 4, 2017, http://www.catholicherald.co.uk/.

2. C.S. Lewis, *Reflections on the Psalms* (New York: Harcourt, Brace & Co., 1958), 93-97.

3. Joseph Cardinal Ratzinger, *The Spirit of the Liturgy* (San Francisco: Ignatius Press, 2014), 43.

4. Thomas à Kempis, *The Imitation of Christ* (Mineola, NY: Dover, 2003), 86.

5. Thomas Aquinas, *Summa Theologica* I.10.

6. Josephus, *Antiquities* 3.8.9.

7. Aaron was clothed at God's command; Adam was clothed with garments by God (Exodus 28:42; Genesis 3:21). The high priests' garments were arrayed with gold and onyx; so too is there mention of gold and onyx in Eden (Exodus 25:7; Genesis 2:11-12). As Aaron cannot draw near to God with his nakedness exposed, so too, after the fall, Adam cannot draw near to God with his nakedness exposed (Genesis 3:10; Exodus 20:26, 28:42).

8. St. Thomas Aquinas, Hebr 8, 4.

9. The order of events is not especially clear. It seems this episode may have occurred within days of their leaving Egypt, before the family priesthood was laicized after the gold calf incident and given to Aaron and the Levites, making it a direct attack on Moses' priesthood as head of the family. Either way, the attack was on God's authority and is presented as such.

10. Edith Stein, "Essays on Woman: Vocations of Man and Woman," in *Collected Works of Edith Stein*, 2nd rev. ed. (Washington, DC: ICS Publications, 1996), 79, 83, 84.

11. Ibid.

12. John L. Allen, Jr., "Why Pope Francis Won't Let Women Become Priests," *Time*, time.com, March 2015.

13. R. Cessario, *Magnificat Magazine*, September 12, 2017, 156.

14. Fulton J. Sheen, *Life Is Worth Living* (San Francisco: Ignatius, 1999), 49-51.

15. (Epist. 40, v). St. Cyprian of Carthage: "Letters," 39, 5. (c. 200 – Sept. 14, 258).

16. Clement, *Letter to the Corinthians*, 1, 44.

17. St. Ignatius, *Letter to the Smyrnaeans*, 8.

18. St. Ignatius, *Letter to the Smyrnaeans*, 9.

19. St. Ignatius, *Letter to the Trallians*, 2-3, 7.

20. *Catholic Encyclopedia,* s.v. "Bartholomew Holzhauser," newadvent.org, accessed August 30, 2017.

21. *Didache*, 9-10.

22. Ibid.

23. *Catena Aurea,* Matthew 5:13, Jerome.

24. Rabbi Ken Spiro, "History Crash Course #12: The Golden Calf," aish.com, accessed August 2017.

25. *Catholic Encyclopedia*, s.v. "Jehovah (Yahweh)," newadvent.org, accessed June 25, 2016.

26. (Mag. 7:2).

27. Cf. Lk 8:13-15; Acts 14:22; Rom 5:3-5; 2 Tim 3:12.

28. Cf. Jas 1:14-15.

29. Origen, De orat. 29 PG 11, 544CD.

30. St. Gregory the Great, Dial. 4, 39: PL 77, 396; cf. Mt 12:31.

31. Susan Tassone, "Purifying the Soul on Earth Is Worth Hundreds of Times What It Takes After," spiritdaily.net/catherinegenoa, accessed December 11, 2017.

32. *Diary of Saint Maria Faustina Kowalska: Divine Mercy in My Soul*, 3rd ed. (Stockbridge, MA: Marian Press, 2005), 20.

33. St. Francis de Sales, quoted in Gerard J.M. van den Aardweg, *Hungry Souls: Supernatural Visits, Messages, and Warnings from Purgatory* (Charlotte, NC: TAN Books, 2012), xxiii.

34. Pope Gregory, quoted in St. Augustine, *De Civ. Dei* i, 8.

35. Gregory of Nyssa, *De iis qui in fide dormiunt*, quoted in *Summa Theologica* Supplement (Appendix II) on Purgatory, Article 1, newadvent.org, accessed December 11, 2017.

36. Cf. Council of Lyons II (1274):DS 857-858; Council of Florence (1439):DS 1304-1306; Council of Trent (1563):DS 1820.]

37. Cf. Benedict XII, *Benedictus Deus* (1336): DS 1000-1001; John XXII, Ne super his (1334): DS 990.

38. Cf. Benedict XII, Benedictus Deus (1336):DS 1002.

39. St. John of the Cross, *Dichos* 64.

40. Benedict XVI, "General Audience: Paul VI Audience Hall: Wednesday, 12 January 2011," w2.vatican.va, accessed December 2011.

41. John Henry Newman, *The Dream of Gerontius*, ccel.org, accessed December 4, 2017, Part 5.

42. W.H. Vanstone, *The Stature of Waiting* (Harrisburg, PA: Morehouse Publishing, 2006).

43. *Catena Aurea, St. Luke – Vol. II*, Luke 22, Bede.

44. St. Ambrose, *de Sacramentis*, lib. v. c. 1 in *The Great Commentary of Cornelius À Lapide: I. Corinthians*, ed. and trans. W.F. Cobb (London: John Hodges, 1896), 228-229.

45. Tertullian, de Baptismo, c. ix in *The Great Commentary of Cornelius À Lapide: Volumes 1 to 8*, trans. Thomas W. Mossman (Aeterna Press, 2014).

46. *Roman Catechism* II, 2, 5; Cf. Council of Florence: DS 1314; CIC, cann. 204 § 1; 849; CCEO, can. 675 § 1.

47. Cf. Council of Trent (1547): DS 1545; *LG* 40.

48. Jerome, *Against Jovinian* 2:30.

49. St. Augustine of Hippo, *Sermon to Catechumens, on the Creed*, in *The Faith of the Early Fathers* Vol. III, ed. and trans. W.A. Jurgens (Collegeville: MN: The Liturgical Press, 1979), 35.

50. *Laudato Si'* 246.

51. Exodus 38:8, 1 Samuel 2:22, 2 Maccabees 3:19-20; Josephus mentions the cloisters in *The Wars of the Jews* 5.5. The Babylonian Talmud says these women wove the temple veils each year and baked the Presence Bread: Atenebris

Adsole ("Babylonian Talmud: Tractate Kethuboth: Folio 106a and Kethuboth 106b," come-and-hear.com, accessed September 2017).

52. Josephus, *Antiquities* 3.8.9.

53. Tertullian, circa 155–240.

54. *CD* 2 § 2.

55. John Paul II, "Letter of His Holiness John Paul II to All the Priests on the Occasion of Holy Thursday 1979," w2vatican.va, accessed August 2017.

56. St. Teresa of Calcutta, *Jesus, The Word to Be Spoken* (Cincinnati, OH: Servant Publications, St. Anthony Messenger Press, 1998), 76.

57. *DV* 10 § 2.

58. St. Ignatius, *Letter to the Smyrnaeans* 6:2–7:1.

59. Benedict XVI, "Homily of His Holiness Benedict XVI: St Peter's Basilica: Fourth Sunday of Easter, 3 May 2009," w2.vatican.va, accessed December 6, 2017).

60. *Didache*, 9:4.

61. Justin Martyr, *First Apology*, 65-67.

62. Ibid., 66.

63. Joseph Mercola, "Why Smells Can Trigger Strong Memories," articles.mercola.com, August, 2015.

64. Pope Francis, "Address of Holy Father Francis: St. Peter's Square: Friday, 31 May 2013," w2.vatican.va, accessed December 2017.

65. Ibid.

66. Find tutorials, audio and video teachings, and resources on LOVE the Word™ at biblestudyevangelista.com.

67. *LG* 11.

68. Jennifer Viegas, "Quake reveals day of Jesus' crucifixion, researchers believe," nbcnews.com, May 2012.

69. Arendzen, J. (1908). "Cherubim," *The Catholic Encyclopedia* (New York: Robert Appleton Company), accessed December 5, 2017 from www.newadvent.org/.

70. *Newman Reader – Works of John Henry Newman* (Pittsburgh, PA: The National Institute for Newman Studies, 2007), Part III, Meditations on Christian Doctrine, A Short Visit to the Blessed Sacrament before Meditation http://www.newmanreader.org, accessed December 2017.

71. John Paul II, *Redemptor Hominis* 10.

72. Carl E. Olson, "The Dignity of the Human Person: Pope John Paul II's Teaching on Divinization in the Trinitarian Encyclicals," *Saint Austin Review* (2002), discussing CCC 460.

73. John Henry Newman, "Meditation of the Day," Morning Offerings, February 14, 2016.

74. Jewish Encyclopedia, s.v. "Gerizim, Mount," jewishvirtuallibrary. org, accessed August 2017.

75. Rev 21:3.

76. "Occam's razor, also spelled Ockham's razor, also called law of economy or law of parsimony, principle stated by the Scholastic philosopher William of Ockham (1285–1347/49)

that *pluralitas non est ponenda sine necessitate*, "plurality should not be posited without necessity." The principle gives precedence to simplicity: of two competing theories, the simpler explanation of an entity is to be preferred. The principle is also expressed as "Entities are not to be multiplied beyond necessity" (Encyclopaedia Britannica, s.v. "Occam's razor," Britannica.com, accessed December 2017).

77. S. Hippolytus, *In Dan.* vi., Patr. Gr., Tom. 10, p. 648.

78. S. Ephrem, *Rhythm* iii., *On the Nativity*, Morris, p. 20.

79. St. Cyril, *De ador. In Spir. Et Verit*, p. 293.

80. Serm. xlii. 6, Int. Opp., S. Ambrosii.

81. Orat. In Deip. Annuntiat, nn. 13, 14. Int. Opp. S. Athanasii and Homily of the Papyrus of Turin.

82. Blessed Columba Marmion, *Christ, the Life of the Soul,* (Tacoma, WA: Angelico Press, 2012), 340.

83. *Providentissimus Deus,* Leo XIII, encyclical, 1893, 38.

84. Dave Armstrong, ed., *The Quotable Newman: A Definitive Guide to His Central Thoughts and Ideas* (Manchester, NH: Sophia Institute Press, 2012), 169.

85. *Mulieris Dignitatem* (On the Dignity and Vocation of Women), John Paul II, apostolic exhortation, 1988.

ABOUT THE AUTHOR

Sonja Corbitt is a vital Catholic voice—an accomplished author, speaker, and broadcaster—who produces high-impact, uplifting multimedia Bible studies. A North Carolina native who was raised as a Southern Baptist, Corbitt converted to the Catholic Faith and served as director of religious education at St. John Vianney Catholic Church in Gallatin, Tennessee, and as executive director of Risen Radio in Lebanon, Tennessee.

She is the host of the *Bible Study Evangelista Show.* Corbitt is in formation as a Third Order Carmelite, is a columnist at *The Great Adventure Bible Study* blog, a contributor to *Magnificat,* and author of *Unleashed, Fearless, Ignite,* and *Fulfilled,* Ascension's two-part study Bible study that this book complements.

She lives in Tennessee with her husband, Bob, with whom she home schools two sons.